Never Wear Pants Again

Why so many businesses won't survive the
pandemic and how remote working will
ensure you make it.

Website In 5 Days LLC
555 Saturn Blvd Suite B605
San Diego CA 92154

Copyright © 2020 by Chris Martinez

First Edition, 2020

DUDE® and Bridge, Connect, and Deliver® are registered
Trademarks of Website In 5 Days, LLC

Designed by Flor Gonzalez
Manufactured in the United States of America

Library of Congress Cataloging in Publication Data

Martinez, Chris R.
Never Wear Pants Again: Why so many businesses
won't survive the pandemic and how remote working
will ensure you make it.

ISBN

978-0-578-78412-0

*For Uncle Joe, Yolanda, and the 1 Million+ people
who have lost their lives to Covid-19.*

Table of Contents

PART 1:
WE DID THIS TO OURSELVES

Chapter 1 .... Pag. 1
The New Normal

>   The Day the World Changed.
>   How the world is changed forever.
>   Why we're not going back.
>   What the future will hold and how to prepare.

Chapter 2 .... Pag.17
We Created These Problems Inside the Home

>   Human Nature and the Path of Least Resistance.
>   The Origins of the "I'm Special Complex" in America.
>   Public Policy and Boosting Self Esteem.

Chapter 3 .... Pag. 27
Ambiguity: The Secret Killer of American Society

>   The Importance of Dealing with Ambiguity.
>   Why dealing with ambiguity is the key to (remote) work success.
>   Traits of the Ambiguously Inept.
>   How to manage someone who can't deal with ambiguity.

Chapter 4 .... Pag. 35
The (De) Evolution of American Society

>   Changes to White America and Their Economy since 1980.
>   Changes and Fears for White Americans.
>   The Psychology Behind Entitlement and the Spoiled American.
>   Things Americans feel entitled to and their origins.
>   Why Entitlement Leads to Inflexibility and Refusal to Change.

Chapter 5 .... Pag. 45
The Four Types of Customers in a Crisis.

>   The Rescue Seeker.
>   The Drowner.
>   The Proof Seeker.
>   The Hungry.

PART 2
TIME TO CHANGE YOUR PANTS

Chapter 6 .... Pag. 53
The Dangers of the Language

The Impact of Language on Behavior.
Internal vs External culture.
Infighting and How it Will Kill Your Company Culture.
How to fix the In-house vs Remote Dilemma.

Chapter 7 ....Pag. 69
Remote Team Members vs Virtual Assistants

Why Everyone will be Remote.
Differences between Remote and Virtual.
5 Benefits of Remote Team Members.
5 Downsides of Remote Team Members.

Chapter 8 ....Pag. 87
How to Succeed in a Remote World

Bridge, Connect, and Deliver®
Daily Deadline Meetings.
Daily communication/status updates for all new clients.

Chapter 9 ....Pag. 95
How to Build Company Culture in a Remote World

How to Make 1000 Miles Away Feel Intimate.
KPIs when Managing a Remote Team.
Best Practices for Maintaining Company Culture.
Red Flags that will Kill Your Culture.

Chapter 10 ....Pag. 111
Deliver Amazing Customer Experiences
with Your Remote Team

Delivering Virtual "Hugs" to your clients.
How most companies get it "wrong".
Managing the "Red Zone."
How to Get Remote Team Members to Obsess About.
Clients They Will Never Meet.

Part 3
Ditch Your Pants

Chapter 11 ....Pag. 129
The New Customer Experience

Why the First 60-days Are So Crucial with Remote Companies.
The 60-Day New Client Journey.
How to Get Clients to Obey the Rules.
Why You Must Have a Customer Experience Director.
What does a Customer Experience Director Do.
How to Find a Customer Experience Director.
Customer Experience Director Job Description.
How to Find One and What to Pay.

Chapter 12...Pag. 157
The Winners and Losers

The Zero-Sum Game of Remote Work.
Who Will Win.
Who Will Lose.
How to ensure you are a CHAMPION.

Chapter 13...Pag. 169
Pants are overrated anyway

5 Things You MUST DO in the Next 30 Days.
The people you need on your team.
Project Manager Job Description.
The people you need to let go.
Taking the ship to Mars.

Bibliography

Foreword

In 2015, I decided to change everything about my life. I had anticlimactically ended a decade-long career as a creative agency owner. And I was looking ahead for a new way to approach the next chapter:

- *I wanted to build an online business.*
- *I wanted to build a remote team.*
- *I wanted to disrupt my industry.*
- *And most of all, I wanted to figure out how to pull it all together with meaning and purpose presiding over marketing and profits.*

With this in mind I set out on a new journey with a business called Design Pickle. And today, we sit at the top of our market for flat-rate creative services. We serve thousands of clients in dozens of countries, and 2020 has been our best year ever.

What I didn't know at the time, but would soon discover, is I wasn't the only one on this journey. Frustrated with the current models and mindsets, there were others working on a new path for themselves to increase their impact on the world.

Chris Martinez was one of these guys. He found himself on a similar trajectory not too far from my hometown of Scottsdale, AZ. Through the years we'd cross paths many times and eventually become close friends. One unforgettable moment in my relationship with Chris was when he brought luchador wrestling to the top United States marketing conference. While others were in slacks and collared shirts, Chris and his team were unapologetically clad in masks and spandex. Today I have the honor to write the forward of his equally unforgettable book.

What you're about to read is not easy. It will challenge you. If you're looking for a quick how-to, a "hack", or anything that requires only a little bit of work to achieve big changes, this is not the book for you. Please put it down now.

Instead, if you're looking to be challenged—not just in the way you approach business, but in the way you approach life—Chris will more than deliver.

Never Wear Pants Again is an all-encompassing journey starting with information on how we arrived in our current business climate and ending with a practical look at the steps Chris has taken to build a thriving business. He takes you behind the curtain on his truly unique worldview and how he has applied it to a bulletproof business model. And he has accomplished all this despite facing the greatest challenges we've seen in any of our lifetimes.

Does he get into the nitty-gritty? Absolutely. But he does it in a radically honest way. He doesn't pull punches, and this is the beauty of Chris. He lives every day with his heart on his sleeve. And through this radical candor, Chris can break the complicated down into the practical.
Despite Chris's recommendation, I still wear pants. But after reading his book, I, too, have come away with new insights and clarity on how to best optimize the insane global climate ahead.

Buckle up. You're about to go on quite a journey. And if you lose your pants in the process, it's actually a good thing. :)

Russ Perry
Founder and CEO of Design Pickle

2 October 2020

Introduction

This goes without saying, but we live in a pretty fucked up time. Millions of people have gotten sick, hundreds of thousands have died, thousands of businesses are gone, and people feel more divided and alone than ever before. If you're like me, then you might be wondering how in the hell we got here.

Truth be told, I've seen this coming for years. Not necessarily the pandemic, but I knew that something major would happen that would alter the way the world works. Some people have called Covid-19 a "black swan" or something that few people saw coming. Bill Gates and some of the world's top epidemiologists definitely saw this coming a long time ago, which is a hallmark of black swans. They are only black swans to those who don't expect them. Since I anticipated that something devastating was coming, I was able to prepare as best I could, and I've actually been able to grow our company while so many people have gone belly up.

When I started writing this book I was going in a totally different direction. I wanted to talk strictly about best practices for remote working and all the tactics that have helped my company to succeed. However, as I started digging into the research I saw that there was something much bigger in play. The effects of Covid-19 on the economy and on the American culture as a whole are really the end results of decades, yes DECADES, of a social and psychological evolution that has been taking place in the United States, and what you will read in this book is that Covid-19 didn't really put anyone out of business. If your business is struggling due to the pandemic or you are worried that the pandemic might harm your business, then you need to know that the real threat to your livelihood is a lot closer to home than you think. And I'll show you exactly why and how to prevent yourself from becoming a casualty.

Never Wear Pants Again is broken down into three parts. I believe that if you truly want to solve a problem then you have to really understand its origins, and so the first 5 chapters of the book talk about the social and psychological factors that have created the perfect storm for Covid-19 to cripple our society. The second section I'll go on to discuss the cultural and mindset shifts that all businesses need to adopt if they really want to survive this evolution. And finally, the last section of the book will give you the tactics and specific action items that you must take if you want to "make it" in this new economy.

Make no mistake, we are living in a new economy that I like to call the "Remote Economy" and the old rules no longer apply. Many employees and business owners have not been equipped to survive this latest evolution and it's why they are struggling today or find themselves out of business. Unfortunately for millions of people, it's too late. The remote economy demands new skills and a new mindset and those that are unable to adapt will find themselves struggling to survive economically and emotionally. For the rest of us who are willing and able to adapt and grow in spite of the massive hurdles in front of us, we are still very much in a battle for survival. The world is changing every day, and it will take mental toughness and skill to make it through this evolution.

The best part in all this mess is that if you are adaptable, if you can fight through the pain, and if you implement what I teach you in this book, then you'll have a really good chance of not only surviving but of building a life-changing business. All this instability in the world has opened the doors for millions of people to build fortunes for themselves and to change the world. Then you'll be able to do whatever you want. Including never having to wear pants again.

PART I
WE DID THIS TO OURSELVES

Chapter 1:

We Did This to Ourselves

Chapter 1- The New Normal

This is not the first time people have used the term "The New Normal". We heard it after 9/11, we heard it after the economic crash in 2008, and now we are hearing it again as we all go through Covid-19. How are you responding to this latest New Normal? Are you feeling anxious or afraid? Are you feeling uncertain about your future? Are you paralyzed with fear?

There are a wide range of emotions that people have been experiencing, and I think we can all agree that many are not able to deal with the uncertainty of life at all. Since March, I've been hearing people say things like "When things go back to normal...", but as soon as Covid-19 hit our shores, I knew that that would never happen. Life as you know it prior to March 2020 is never coming back.

Covid-19 is something that has changed the US and the world forever. I tell you this not to make you depressed but so that you can make peace with it and move on. There is no time to wallow in the mud and wish for the "good ol' days" because they aren't coming back, no matter how much you want them to. In this chapter, I'm going to talk in more detail about why I anticipated that something major was about to hit our country, how I've come to peace with this new reality, and what my outlook for the future is.

The Day the World Changed.

It was a normal Saturday morning in Tijuana, Mexico, where I now live as an American Expat in the world's most dangerous city. Like most Saturday mornings, I was sitting around texting my two friends Gary and Travis, giving each other the normal shit-talking banter. I was calling them "weak babies" and "entitled Americans" as I scrolled through video after video of Americans ransacking grocery stores and Costcos across the US in search of toilet paper.

Travis was noticeably annoyed by the irrational fear that was sweeping the nation, but Gary was actually more scared than I had ever seen him before. With two young boys and a wife at home, 4 elderly parents close-by, and two more grandparents 100 miles away, Gary felt like he had a lot to lose. Now taking into consideration his $600k annual salary, Gary could afford to build a bunker in his backyard and hide out for a few years with all his loved-ones, but his emotions were running high and he was very worried that the Coronavirus would somehow sneak into his house (and the houses of his loved-ones) and kill them all.

It's a fear that many Americans had after watching the news around the world and seeing the fatality numbers shoot up like a wicked stock market report. This was unlike any enemy we had ever known because it existed at a microscopic level and killed at random.

For Gary and Travis, living and working in the San Francisco Bay Area, the reality of the pandemic became all too real as the city went into lockdown much sooner than the rest of the country. Fortunately, both worked in software and so their jobs did not require them to go into the office or even be around people. But they still faced those terrifying phrases that all parents dread to hear combined: 'Work From Home' and 'Kids Are Out of School.'

Within 24 hours, both of my friends found themselves part of the "remote workforce". It was a sobering moment for them as employees, but also an eye-opening one for their bosses. How was all this remote working going to actually, for lack of a better word, WORK?

Which brings me back to my original story of us guys talking shit back and forth over our standard Saturday morning texts. I continued badgering Gary while simultaneously texting Travis individually asking if Gary was ok.

- *"Is Gary seriously freaking out about the coronavirus?" I asked via our separate chat.*

- *"Yeah man, he's pretty worried about it." Travis replied.*

For those that are wondering, this is considered a "deep" conversation for guys and is the equivalent of an emotional plea for help.

I wrote a few lines back to the group chat and tried to ease Garys' fears by telling him I didn't think that it was going to be that bad, but in the back of my mind, I knew that this virus would change the world and the way we conduct business forever.

Within days, the Coronavirus altered the way we do business and revealed some massive weaknesses in the economy. At the onset of the pandemic, many folks were wanting to "wait it out" and wondering when "we could return" to normal, while I was the crazy person, shouting that we were NEVER going back to that normal.

Well guess who was right?

THIS GUY.

That's the beauty of being able to look at the world through the eyes of an outsider. You get to see things coming that nobody else can see. I refer to it as being the dog that can see the rainbow. Dogs are colorblind, but one day, one dog came along and told all the other dogs to look up to the sky so they could see the beautiful rainbow above. Every time it rained, this special dog told all the others to stare at the sky and wait for the beautiful rainbow with all its pretty colors to appear. Unfortunately all the other dogs just thought he was crazy. (I actually got this analogy from some really bad movie starring Meg Ryan and Hugh Jackman)

My point is that, while all this was going on, I was able to prepare my own business and our clients for the big lockdown so that we were able to not only survive the pandemic but to THRIVE. Looking back, the single biggest keys to our success were to embrace the philosophy that remote workers (aka VAs) are just as important as in-house staff and to create a customer experience that completely "wow'd" our clients no matter where they were. We created processes to survive in a remote world, and because of this, our clients and our own business actually got STRONGER during the shutdown.

On March 20, 2020, my company took the stance that we would quarantine our staff and work from home 3 weeks prior to the government mandates here in Mexico. We had the structures in place to work remotely and we had tested these processes multiple times before, so we decided to close our office indefinitely. It was a somber day for us because we had no idea when we would be able to see each other again, but the primary objective was to keep our staff safe and reduce the chance of infection. Most people don't know that Mexico has one of the highest rates of obesity and diabetes in the world, and so not only are they at higher risk of death, the culture itself makes it much harder to socially distance. With this in mind, we had to be super aggressive in closing our doors and constantly remind our staff to stay the fuck home.

As the Coronavirus began to spread throughout Tijuana and hospitals began to fill up with patients, our proactive approach seemed to be working. None of our staff got sick, and our business flourished. We saw record client retention numbers while also seeing a massive increase in new business, meaning we were experiencing a boom in business that we hadn't seen in years. For all intents and purposes, the Covid-19 pandemic has been one of the best things to happen to our business as well as to our clients.

Make no mistake, what we experienced during the first lockdown is not the exception to the rule. Much like 9/11 changed air travel forever, Covid-19 has changed the way we do business forever. I anticipate that soon over-priced commercial real estate offices with open floor plans and come-as-you-are policies will disappear. In fact, potential employees will actually look DOWN on the fact that you don't have a more regulated work environment with work-from-home options. Yes, there will still be a need for people to come together, but instead of working from home being the exception, it will now become the rule.

You the business owner, whether you be a digital agency owner, a banker, a construction company, or a police chief need to learn how to adapt to this new way of doing business. Remote work is here to stay so you only have two options.

Adapt.

Or die.

How the world is changed forever.

One of the things that has bothered me the most throughout this entire pandemic is the overwhelming rhetoric from both sides about the economy being "shutdown". At first, it was a term of security as if we have locked down our house to protect ourselves, but eventually "locked down" turned into a feeling of helplessness, restriction, and financial slavery. Yet nobody ever challenged this notion of "economic lockdown". You were either "for it" or you were "against it". You were either for "liberating" or "lockdown".

Were we ever really locked down, though?

Did credit card processing machines stop working? Did ATM machines stop spitting out money? Did the government reach into your bank account and prevent you from collecting money from your customers?

The answer to all these questions is a resounding "no", but what DID change is the way that companies conducted their business and the way that customers exchanged money for services.

Somehow we Americans had become so spoiled as a society that we believed there was only one way to do business. We believed that if you wanted to work out in a gym, you had to buy a membership, walk over to where all the machines were, and sweat your ass off alongside all those other people. If you wanted to go to a dentist, we believed that you had to call, make an appointment, sit in the waiting room with a bunch of strangers, then go sit in another room with a funny chair, and finally a masked man would come in and look at your grill and tell you if you needed to give him a shit ton of money to fix your busted mouth. If you needed your carpets cleaned, we believed that you had to call some stranger to come to your house, enter your home with his filthy shoes, do some arbitrary calculations, then drag his filthy equipment into your house to essentially vacuum your filthy carpet with hot water and soap.

It's the way we've been doing business for centuries. One person walks in to meet another person, they talk and negotiate, and then one person leaves with money for services rendered. And USUALLY both parties are happy.
The question I ask is, "WHY????"

Why in the world have we conducted business like this?

An astounding 78% of the American workforce was working in an office prior to the pandemic, which means that 78% of Americans were somehow tied to this cycle of person-to-person commerce. It didn't matter what stage of the sale you were in, your physical presence was required for legal tender to be exchanged.

For the 22% that were able to work from home or work remotely, we were seen as the black sheep of the economy. How could we possibly get work done without going to an office? I've actually heard people dismiss remote work, saying they would never be able to work from home because they couldn't focus or would have too many distractions.

Now if you have a bunch of kids running around the house I understand, but at the end of the day, we are all paid to solve problems so figuring out how to do your job from home is just another problem you have to solve. Throwing up your hands and giving up is just not an option.

What the pandemic revealed to us is that the old way of commerce is not necessarily the only way anymore. It accelerated the evolution that had started with the very first ecommerce purchase way back in 1994. Slowly but surely, the world has been adapting to a remote and virtual marketplace. You read the news every year about department stores closing, retail sales are down, print publications are dying, etc, etc, etc.

Yet like the ostrich with its head in the sand, many Americans arrogantly sat there and thought to ourselves "well, this could never happen to MY industry! I am technology proof!"

What's that Bible verse they teach you growing up?

Oh yeah.

"Pride goeth before a fall."

This is exactly what happened with Covid-19. Decades of pride and a collective ignorance towards the vulnerability of our business culture set the stage for a dramatic downfall, and within a couple weeks, we had 30 million people unemployed and hundreds of thousands of businesses closing their doors for good.

As much as it pains me to say it, the closing of all those businesses was exactly the purge that we needed. Business is evolution only, in business, it's not the strongest that survive but the ones who are the quickest to adapt to change. I'm willing to bet that if you really look hard at the companies that went under right after Covid-19 hit the U.S, you would find that 99% of those businesses did not have the basic digital infrastructure to survive. Things like a website that generates leads from the internet, online ordering and payment processing, online document signing, and video consultations.

There are thousands of organizations that can help you set up and run your business remotely and they have been around for a long time. There is literally no excuse why you could not have set up some contingency plan, so that if you weren't able to physically open your doors and see your customers, you still couldn't make it. Don't believe me? These technologies have been around for years and they cost very little money to implement. Here is a list of companies that help normal brick-and-mortar companies conduct business virtually:

- YouTube, Founded 2005
- Zoom, Founded 2011
- DocuSign, Founded 2003
- Kajabi, Founded 2010
- LeadPages, Founded 2008
- WordPress, Founded 2003
- Stripe, Founded 2009
- Paypal, Founded 1998

With these tools you can literally run 99.999% of small businesses from anywhere in the world. And there are thousands of other software companies out there that are more industry-specific and can enable you to run YOUR business 10x better than how you are doing it today.

So why did so many small businesses fall apart at the first sign of the pandemic?

Arrogance and stupidity.

There I said it. It might not be the nice thing to say, but it is God's honest truth. And now that the world has been pushed to the next evolution, there is no turning back. We've gotten a taste for the remote workforce economy, and we are flat-out not going back, so get it through your head and tell everyone you know.

Life is NEVER going back to the way it was back in January 2020. Never. Ever, ever, ever, ever going back. NEVER.

Secondly, the economy was never "shutdown". You just had to show your customers a new way to do business with you. Plain and simple. Those that got creative and figured this out early succeeded, and those that did not faltered or failed. This is why I love capitalism in 2020 because evolutions are taking place so fast that one day you might be the zebra and the next you might be the lion.

When 9/11 happened and you had to take off your shoes and your belt, then go through the scanners that displayed your tiny dick to TSA, and then finally show your ID and boarding pass to 3 more people before getting on that plane, it was a huge inconvenience... for about 6 minutes. Then you just kind of got used to it. Now nobody complains about the longer lines and more precautions because at the end of the day all the sacrifices are worth it since we don't have to worry about some terrorist flying our plane into a building.

This pandemic will be just like that. Right now, people are losing their damn minds, but when Karen realizes she can't get her pumpkin spice latte without wearing a mask, she'll put it back on. When companies realize they don't need those massive offices anymore, they aren't going to bring people in anymore.

And in 20 years time, assuming that we haven't killed each other, remote working won't be A thing, it will be THE thing.

Why we're not going back

The first rule of this evolution is that we are never going back to the way things were before.

The second rule of evolution is that we are NEVER GOING BACK TO THE WAY THINGS WERE BEFORE.

But maybe you are still asking why I'm telling you this after all the evidence I just gave you?

Fair enough. I understand that people learn in different ways so I'll just break it down for you in a different way.

When you look at the publicly traded technology companies that I mentioned before, let's look at their stock prices in November 2019 which is approximately one month prior to the pandemic breaking out in China.

- YouTube/Alphabet $1273.74/share
- Zoom, $70.39
- DocuSign, $66.88
- Paypal, $104.98

Now let's look at their stock prices in late September 2020.

- YouTube/Alphabet $1444.61
- Zoom, $496.50
- DocuSign, $212.36
- Paypal, $187.25

On the flip side, commercial real estate is about to get hammered in the US when companies realize that they no longer need to have all their staff in the office to be productive. Did you know that the average company spends 20% of its gross revenue on office space? Twenty fricken percent.

Companies do this because they think business can only be conducted with the big fancy office space, with all the people jibber jabbering in the office, with the endless birthday cakes and the awkward happy hours where Mike from accounting gets too drunk and sexualy harasses all the women in the office.

I'm not saying that we should do away with working from the office altogether. In fact, I still plan on having my staff work from the office in a much smaller capacity after the pandemic is over because I love when our team members are together and can fulfill the basic human need for face-to-face interaction. What I am definitely saying though is that you need to be nimble enough to operate in both spaces. Too many companies were a one-trick pony and were crushed when they couldn't adapt to the remote economy.

Now we have technology companies that are helping businesses operate in a virtual economy, and those tech companies are killing it because the really smart people on this planet know that Covid-19 was the catalyst we have all been waiting for. These are the facts. This is what is happening right now. Look at who the big winners were back when 9/11 happened. The travel website, Priceline.com, had a single-digits stock price in 2001; now it's worth over $1500/share. The world is going digital, and if you follow the money, you will see that there is no stopping this train. Just buckle up and enjoy the ride.

What the future will hold and how to prepare

So where do we go from here?

This is literally the billion dollar question.

As of right now in the US, just over 2% of the population has been diagnosed as having or had the Covid-19 virus. That 2% meant major consequences to the economy, more than 200,000 deaths in 6 months time, and immeasurable psychological damage to the majority of the population.

Offices in all 50 states were closed and everyone was forced to figure out how to survive the pandemic both physically and financially. In the meantime, scientists, doctors, and mathematicians are working around the clock to try and predict what is going to happen next, which is incredibly difficult since we have never had a Coronavirus pandemic quite like this one. To the outside observer, it appears that the people steering the ship have absolutely no idea what they are doing, but to the trained eye, the uncertainty and constant change of direction is inevitable when dealing with such a complex adversary.

But that 2% of Americans who were diagnosed with Covid-19 was just the tip of the iceberg. Unless a vaccine can be proven effective, approved, and manufactured for global distribution to 7.2 Billion people within the next 18-24 months, it is very likely that the virus will continue to decimate lives and change the way that we live. Without extreme social distancing, somewhere around 200 million Americans are expected to contract the Covid-19 virus within the next 18 months, and between 800,000 to 1.6 million are expected to die from Covid-19 related illnesses if a vaccine can not be brought to the marketplace quick enough.

Part of the reason why this virus is so hard to contain is because we do not have any public policy in place to handle this type of respiratory disease. According to Dr. Michael Osterholm from the University of Minnesota, Covid-19 is like a "leaky bucket virus" in that if there is a single little crack anywhere, the virus will get out and more people will become infected, starting the cycle all over again.[1] On one hand, reaching herd immunity at 60-70% infection for the total population will signal that we are out of the woods. But on the other hand getting to that point means that many, many hundreds of thousands of people need to die. Those people are our mothers and fathers, our friends, our sons and daughters, and many others who influence our lives every single day.

While nobody knows when the virus will cease to be a problem in the world, we do know that one way or another it will eventually stop terrorizing our planet. The biggest upside to all of this is that from an economical standpoint, we are much more in control of our destiny. There is no "herd immunity" for businesses, and we do not need to wait for a vaccine to protect ourselves from this or any virus' effects for that matter. We are much more in the driver's seat when it comes to how we let Covid-19 impact our financial well-being.

When we look at the first three months of the pandemic here in the US and the companies that did well versus the companies that did poorly or went out of business, those that had a nimble workforce who already knew how to work remotely are the ones that survived.

Plain and simple.

The companies who were slow to move and could not adapt their labor force to a remote economy suffered and/or died. While there are some industries that require people maintain a close proximity to each other (like professional football), the overwhelming number of industries can absolutely operate remotely if they adjust some of the ways they conduct their business and implement a combination of technology and automation.

Think about it, a house painter can provide quotes virtually, social distance and sanitize everything in the client's home while performing the job, and collect payment through an online portal. A manufacturing plant can separate workers with protective barriers, adjust their assembly lines to include more robot automation where it's too dangerous to have humans close together, and then even use robot delivery drivers to ship their products.

Many people who don't like change and don't understand business will complain that this is killing jobs, but the reality is that when one job ends, another is created. That is the beauty of evolution. The old makes way for the new, and death opens the door for new life. When a zebra is killed by a pack of lions, the entire pride feeds off the meat from the zebra, allowing more cubs to mature and eventually produce their own offspring. Furthermore, the decaying carcass from the zebra nurtures the soil, fertilizing new grass that then feeds future zebras. I bet you can hear the "Circle of Life" song playing in your head right now!

If you want to be the lion in this analogy and not the zebra, then you must have a nimble and scalable workforce that can work remotely. To put that another way, you need a REMOTE WORKFORCE and the processes to get that team to perform even better than when they were together in an office. Literally any business (including the NFL) can do this, but it will often mean massive technological and automation changes to your business, but it is definitely possible to survive and thrive using these tactics.

The best part is that I'll show you exactly how to do that in this book, starting with abandoning all your past misconceptions of why remote work is impossible for you and then helping you transform your mindset so that your company can prosper in the virtual economy. No Covid-19 virus will be able to stop you! No "economic shutdown" will stand in your way! Your business will become invincible!!!

Chapter 2

We Created These Problems Inside the Home

I love a good backstory. Whether it be in a book or a movie, I love to learn WHY things are the way they are. Initially, I was going to make this book all tactics, but I feel like it's important for everyone to understand why the transition from in-house to remote has become such a challenge for many Americans. The culprit is not that some people are more technologically-inclined or that some have more money to implement new gadgets. The problem is ideology. Many Americans simply refuse to change their ways. The internet has been around for almost 30 years and yet 36% percent of businesses still do not have a fucking website. It's so unbelievably easy to get a website today, and you can even get one for free in many cases. These people refuse to play the game with their lack of creativity or innovation, and this isn't just a small group of lagards. These are thousands of businesses and millions of people.

In this chapter, I'm going to paint a very detailed picture as to WHY so many people are so unbelievably stubborn and cannot adapt, not just to remote work but to any type of change. We will focus on the psychological and sociological impacts that parenting styles played in creating all the chaos and issues that we have today. It is my belief that an educated population will be a population who makes better decisions, so with the lessons in this chapter, I hope that you prove me right.

Human Nature and the Path of Least Resistance

Disgraced comedian Louis CK has a joke that I love. He talks about when you're sitting at a light and some asshole realizes at the last minute that they have to turn left and they end up blocking the entire street for everyone else. Even though all the people behind that person are honking and cursing, the person in the car just throws their hands up as if to say "but what am I supposed to do??? This is MY WAYYYY!!!" They are completely unwilling to go up one block and then take a slightly altered route from their original course.

In many ways, this describes American society today. We have become so entitled as a nation that any deviation from our "normal way" feels like an attack on our Constitutional freedom. Don't get me wrong. I still believe that the United States is the greatest country on Earth and that there is more economic opportunity in America than anywhere else. But after living in Mexico for several years, I've realized many of America's shortcomings and some new American values that might undermine our great republic.

Americans have been shouting "We're #1!" for so long that we haven't stopped to question if it's actually true. The majority of Americans have stopped questioning everything from our healthcare system to the prices we pay for food and many in our society arrogantly assume that the American way must automatically be the best way. I was lucky that my father taught me to always question authority and the status quo. Consequently, I am always trying to see if there is another way to do things or learn from someone who has a better way. This has become one of my superpowers and has helped me to see things that many others can't.

The reason why Americans continue to believe that we always know best is because it's the easiest thing to believe. Think about it. What is easier? Questioning that everything you know and believe is wrong, or continuing the rhetoric that you've been told your entire life? Human beings take the path of least resistance and in this instance, the path of least resistance is staying the course and believing that everything American is better than anything foreign.

Critical thinking is hard. Having your own opinions is hard. Diverging from the status quo is not the path of least resistance. The great thing about the Coronavirus pandemic is that it shocked us into questioning everything. Suddenly everyone, including those who clung to the status quo, were forced to find a new path. We have all had to re-evaluate our priorities and our beliefs. We have been forced to change the way we interact with other humans and the way we conduct commerce. So from that perspective, the Coronavirus has been one of the greatest propellants for our species in the last 100 years.

Pressure, as they say, creates diamonds and our society is about to evolve into a precious gem.

The Origins of the "I'm Special Complex" in America

Over the past 50 years, there have been many shifts in American culture. While the overwhelming majority of those changes have been great for society and have paved the way for the innovations and comforts that we enjoy today, some of these changes have led to serious negative side effects that threaten all the advancements we have made as a culture. Of all these negative side effects, the "I'm Special Complex" could be the single biggest factor that undermines American democracy. The shocking thing is that this entire ethos can be traced back to a shift in parenting that started back in the 1980s.

According to Judith Rich Harris author of *The NURTURE ASSUMPTION: Why Children Turn Out the Way They Do*, parenting styles have changed, but children have not.[2] Parents at the turn of the century were more worried about raising spoiled, disobedient, and self-centered children and thus gave little physical affection or praise to their child. Don't get me wrong, there are definitely negative sides to not telling your child you them or are proud of them. But one massive societal benefit that this parenting philosophy birthed was that it led to a generation of children who grew up believing more in the collective "we" as opposed to the individual "me".

As times changed after World War II and the War in Vietnam, the advice from parenting gurus shifted and thus so did the parenting styles that were being advocated. If you were to pinpoint when the shift solidified, in 1984 Heidi Murkoff and Sharon Mazel published the book *"What to Expect When You're Expecting"* and changed the American-style of parenting forever. Murkoff and Mazel's book was criticized by many scientific experts for promoting paranoia and fear among new mothers, which had never been promoted at such scale prior to this book being published. To date Murkoff and Mazel have sold more than 20 million copies of *"What to Expect When You're Expecting"* and have produced 13 more sequel books. These two authors paved the way for this massive parenting shift. Now parents believe that after their child is born that the child is still in constant danger and that reprimanding children will hurt their self-esteem and harm their belief in themselves later on in life, so parents are reprimanding their children less than the parents did prior to 1984.

What is the result?

Harris believes that instead of creating humans who are less aggressive, more self-confident, kinder, and happier, we've actually seen the complete opposite. According to the results, rates of childhood and adult depression and suicide are up, agression has increased, and I would argue that an over-emphasis on individualism has made it nearly impossible for people to see eye-to-eye on a variety of topics ranging from politics to economics.

It appears that the changes in parenting styles that tried to focus on everyone being special have majorly backfired and now nobody "feels" special.

I specifically remember the age of the "latch-key" kid back in the late 1980s and early 1990s. This was a time when kids were still allowed to walk to school on their own and riding a bike without a helmet was a badge of honor. Shows like "Married with Children" and "Roseanne" almost glorified the rebellious and independent children who would come and go as they please. Unbeknownst at the time, these shows would also signal the eventual downfall of the latch-key children.

While murder and crime rates have dramatically FALLEN since the 1980s and 1990s, media coverage rose dramatically during the 1990s and 2000s regarding child abduction and gun violence.[3] Parents and society in general were being fed lies about the dangers that lay around every corner in American society, which then mutated the already pervasive "my child is special" mantra into "everyone is trying to harm my special child". Many parents believed that their child was the most special creature in the universe and that outside forces were now conspiring to take him/her away from you.

Collective good and doing right by others had no chance against the fear tactics being perpetuated in the mainstream media. Parents now had to watch over their children at all times, giving rise to the "helicopter parents" whose sole purpose was to ensure their child's survival and to keep their child from experiencing any physical or emotional pain in this incredibly dangerous world.

An Oxford University study also found that by the late 1990s there was a dramatic increase in mental health disorders among teenagers and adolescents. In addition, there was an increase in antisocial behavior even though the time that parents and children spent together also INCREASED between the 1980s and 1990s.[4] Researchers believe that since parents were trying to spend more time with their children in an effort to protect them from the dangers of society, that adolescents naturally pushed away, not just from their own parents but also from other teenagers. This created much deeper polarization between children and teens who, in prior generations, were more likely to get along. Yet another indicator of how the "My child is special" belief was backfiring.

The final piece of this puzzle comes from the re-classification of non-working mothers from being called "Housewives" to "Stay-at-home-moms" in the 1990s.[5] Prior to this movement, "housewives" or "homemakers" were tasked with maintaining the home, supporting their husband (who was typically the main breadwinner), and making sure that the children were controlled and presentable if they were ever to be showcased in public. The emphasis of the housewife was the HOME, which made perfect sense since children were still seen as needing to be controlled and raised to be good contributing members of society.

However as gender roles changed and socioeconomic demands shifted, terminology also started to shift in the ways that we looked at the mother within a household. Housewife or homemaker just didn't seem to fit anymore, and mothers all around the United States started to demand more appreciation for their JOB of taking care of the house.

But how could mothers who were not technically being paid for their work finally get the appreciation that they deserved?

Well, since part of her job was to protect her children from the perils of American society....

BOOM! Just like that the term "stay-at-home-mom" took off like wildfire.

Now the "stay-at-home-mom" had a job title that was befitting of the hard work that she was putting in. And on top of that, the shift in her responsibilities went from taking care of the home as a whole to that of safeguarding her precious, unique, and uber-talented little children.

Within less than a decade, the mother's new job title reinforced the belief that the children were of the utmost importance in the family. Even today, you see countless Stay-at-Home-Moms who are forced to hire additional help to take care of the house, because now her main role is to protect and serve her children. Have the actual physical demands of raising children increased? All supporting data suggests that those demands have not, but the societal norms that dictate the court of public perception have definitely altered the way that mothers operate. In the past, children were free to explore the world independently, whereas today you can be thrown in jail for leaving your child unattended.

In the end, little Johnny is made to feel like the world revolves around him...because now it does.

Public Policy and Boosting Self Esteem

In 2020, every American has heard of the importance of building up a child's self esteem, but the reality is that the origin of this concept emerged way back in the 18th Century and modern society has altered its meaning to fit our current state of affairs. In the 1960s, a social psychologist by the name of Morris Rosenberg actually invented a scale that would be used by mental health professionals to gauge people's self esteem: the Rosenberg Self Esteem Scale. RSES became the gold standard for measuring self esteem. It measured the test subject on a scale of 0-40, and anything 15 or less was an indicator that the subject was in danger.[6]

Fast forward to 1986, and while the United States is embroiled in a number of social problems including the war on drugs, a Democratic California Assemblyman by the name of John Vasconcellos decided that he would start a new war. A war on Low Self-Esteem.

Vasconcellos was deeply interested in psychology and believed that most of the problems of the poor and underprivileged could be solved by simply raising their self-esteem. Clearly self-esteem caused their poverty instead of being low because they lived in squalor. But Vasconcellos wouldn't know anything about that. Vasconcellos attended one of the most prestigious private all-boys

prep schools and later one of the most expensive private Jesuit universities on the West Coast. One could easily
argue that Vasconcellos did not really have much in common with the people that he actually aimed to help, but this did not stop him.

Vasconcellos compared an increase in self-esteem to a vaccine that would protect people, especially the underprivileged, from many of life's challenges. He created a task force called the "Task Force on Self-Esteem and Personal and Social Responsibility", which also further increased the legitimacy that the individual was the center of the universe, that there were dangers all around, and that we needed all-hands-on-deck to prevent such a pure and innocent creature from being corrupted by the dangers of the streets and the bad feelings that could infiltrate little Johnny's mind.[7]

More than 10 years later, researchers discovered that Vasconcellos was wrong and that low self-esteem was just a small and almost insignificant factor in battling society's bigger issues. However the damage had already been done for millions of parents and their children.

These problems that were created in the 1980s and 1990s are one of the main reasons we see so many societal issues today. People can't get along. Nobody wants to budge on even the simplest issues. All the worlds' problems are someone else's fault and not mine. And worst of all, our society feels more disconnected and lost than ever before.

Chapter 3

Ambiguity: The Secret Killer of American Society

We just talked about the single-most profound sociological factor to American society's inability to adapt and adjust to change, but this is not the only contributor. A major psychological issue that plagues our society is the increasing number of people who are incapable of handling ambiguity in the world and therefore reject change and more specifically, reject the unknown of the future.

We live in an increasingly uncertain world that is constantly in a state of flux due to globalization and the explosion of technological advancements. At some point, everyone feels the uneasiness and anxiety of not knowing what is about to happen. Whether it's when we are looking for a new job, going on blind dates, or in the midst of a medical emergency. In my instance, nothing was more painful for me than watching my father's diagnosis of stage 4 liver cancer morph into a very aggressive diagnosis of pancreatic cancer that very rapidly ended his life. For the 30 days that he was sick, each day was unbearable because of the ambiguity, of not knowing how much more time we would have with him.

The Importance of Dealing with Ambiguity

Human beings' natural aversion to ambiguity is not always a bad thing. According to Jamie Holmes, author of *Nonscience: The Power of Not Knowing*, ambiguity in our lives can actually be like an "emotional amplifier" if we discover the techniques to unlock this super power.[8] The key differentiator between those who deal with ambiguity well and those who do not comes down to how well the individual is at handling stress. The better someone is at handling stress, the easier it is for that person to use said stressor as a source of power and motivation. On the other hand, if that same person does not have the tools to manage stress, then they will become much more likely to view stress as a negative and will immediately shut down and lose their ability to see their way through or around that ambiguity.

As Holmes explains, 9/11 and the terrorist attacks in the US were major stimuli in America's need to eliminate ambiguity. We can all remember the terror and subsequent fear that came with watching the Twin Towers fall, one-by-one on that sunny autumn day in Manhattan. The entire world came to a crashing halt with no warning, and for the next few years, we didn't know when the next attack was coming, who would be attacking us, and what method they would use to try and murder thousands of innocent people. Nearly 20 years later, the emotional hangover from that experience is still shaping the lives of millions of Americans.

Now think about all the little changes that have happened throughout different parts of the US that have created more ambiguity and uncertainty for its citizens. The Iraq War that eventually turned into the War in Afghanistan. The 2007 financial crisis that saw thousands of people lose their homes and jobs. The 2008 election of America's first black President that created hope for many but apprehension and fear for others. The dominance of internet technologies and e-commerce that has crushed retail businesses and changed the way we do business forever. And most recently, Covid-19 and the global shift against a virus that we still know so little about.

When you combine all of these events, plus the hundreds of other events that have played out on a regional scale within the US, and then combine all this with a generation of adults who were never equipped sufficiently to handle and manage stress, you have essentially created a recipe for disaster. You have the most stressful and ambiguous time in history, thrown in front of a society who is the least equipped to handle it.

No wonder we are all failing.

Why dealing with ambiguity is the key to (remote) work success

From a work standpoint, we have all had those people who are just incapable of coping with change. Hollywood even makes light of those people in movies like "Office Space" where you have Kevin burning the office down because someone stole his red stapler. Or in the show "The Office" with the character Angela who flips out at anything that doesn't seem to fit her personal narrative of how the world is supposed to operate.

These people exist in real life, too. Unfortunately for them, their incapacity to handle change and the unknown in daily life will cause even greater pain as these people are forced to work remotely. Whether you like it or not, the future is and always will be ambiguous. If you have any chance of surviving the remote-work environment shift, then you better learn how to deal with it properly.

There are several key areas that you can focus on to improve your ability to deal with change and uncertainty starting with your ability to take action in uncertain times. This might be one of the biggest challenges for those that aren't used to handling ambiguity as most people feel like they need all the details and data before embarking on a project.

Entrepreneurs are the outliers because they typically take the "ready, fire, aim" approach to life. An entrepreneur sees opportunities where others see obstacles and so in many ways an entrepreneur is hardwired to survive unlike the rest of the population. If you're reading this and you're an entrepreneur, then you probably have these traits inside of you and your goal should be to learn how to harness these super powers properly. Don't act hastily, but instead use your survival instincts to seize the opportunities without overthinking or making hasty decisions.

But for the general population, they need all their ducks in a row before taking the first shot. Part of this comes from a lack of self-confidence, which coincidentally was hindered in most people due to the "boost your kid's self-esteem" movement in the 1980s, 1990s, and 2000s. However, finding the self-assurance to take actions and make decisions based on little data is crucial to thriving in an ambiguous world.

Finally, having great communication skills will make you more adaptable to the new reality because the better you can communicate, the better you will be able to analyze however many facts you do have in front of you.[9] You might only have time to gather 50% of the details you need to make a decision, but if that 50% was communicated effectively, you'll have a much better chance of choosing the right answer.

Traits of the Ambiguously Inept

There are a number of immediate reasons why people are unable to deal with ambiguity in the workplace and it's important to be able to identify them quickly. The following is a list of identifiers that you should look out for[10]:

Not comfortable with change or uncertainty.- Some people actually pride themselves or boast about not being comfortable with change. Whether they say "I don't like change" or through their actions they sabotage efforts to change, you can usually identify these people pretty easily because they don't feel the need to hide this character trait.

May not do well on obscure problems with no clear solution or outcome.- Many people are averse to solving any kind of problems, but especially problems that have no clearly defined right or wrong answers.

May like to have more data than others.- Some people refuse to start a project until they have all the "pieces".

Less efficient and productive under ambiguity.- You might notice that some people are much less productive in a situation where there is lots of ambiguity. If you see that the output is not the same in certain scenarios then this could be the case.

Too quick to close.- Some people will rush to finish a project or determine that a problem is completed before it actually is because they don't like the ambiguity of it.

May like to do things in the same way again and again.- In most positions, you have process managers and project managers. The majority of people are process-driven meaning they like to do things the same way every single time.

How to manage someone who can't deal with ambiguity

While it's simplest to avoid team members who don't do well in intense or uncertain situations, eventually you will need to deal with someone who is incapable of handling ambiguity. Whether it is a boss or a subordinate, one of these people will find their way into your life and you'll either have to fire them or retrain them to adapt.

According to the Harvard Business Review, many of the change-averse inevitably divide the world into two categories: friends and enemies.[11] There is no middle ground and you're either with them or against them. Psychologists call these people "bivalent", and their behavior can often be attributed to traumatic events that occurred when they were younger. Bivalents have a very difficult time understanding that you can hold both positive and negative feelings about someone and thus it contributes to their hatred of ambiguity.

There are two methods for dealing with bivalents. In the event that the bivalent is acting difficult, you will need to schedule time to review the situation with the person, identify different viewpoints, and help the individual see that their way of viewing the situation was not the only way. It is almost as though you'll need to coach the individual on empathy and help them to see the world through the lens of other people.

The second way to handle a bivalent acting out is to have the individual keep a journal where they write down the situations where they feel like someone is acting like an "enemy". Once the individual is aware of and then documents their beliefs, it is much more likely that they will start to question the validity of their beliefs. They will start to see that maybe the world isn't out to get them after all and that maybe they are actually projecting their own insecurities onto others.

Chris Martinez

Chapter 4:

The (De) Evolution of American Society

If you open Facebook, you can see for yourself how severe polarization has taken over the United States over the past 15 years. It seems like the US is on the verge of our next Civil War as families and friends are quickly turning against one another. Since 1980, the United States has experienced a technological revolution not seen since the Industrial Revolution of the late 1800s and early 1900s. The shift in the technology not only created massive changes to the economy, but also changes to the demographic and socioeconomic makeup of the country.

For example, since 1980 the United States service-sector has quadrupled in size from 66 million jobs to 122 million in 2017.[12] However, the manufacturing sector has seen a decline of 5 million jobs during the same time period. Interestingly enough, due to automation the production of goods has actually risen by 80%! That means that productivity has increased but at the expense of factory workers' jobs.

For middle-class American families, commodities like food, clothing, and transportation have gotten less expensive during that time period. However, the cost of a college education, which has always been one of the biggest means for upward social mobility, has gotten incredibly pricey since the early 2000s. Other major expenses like healthcare have also risen dramatically meaning that it's become harder for middle-class Americans to survive and thrive.

In this chapter, we will talk about the exact events and societal shifts that have contributed to these massive cultural and socio-economic divides that we have today. These are real issues that Americans in different walks of life are facing, and they have faced them very differently. After looking at this data, you should be able to see the exact things you need to fix in your business and in your leadership style to thrive in a post-Covid era.

Changes to White America and Their Economy since 1980

Many people like to blame things like Corporate pay and Wall Street greed for the lack of growth in mainstream wages, but a deeper analysis of the data shows that the problem is actually much more closely related to education. In 1979, a person with a college degree would make 38% more money over their lifetime than someone without a college degree. Today, a person with a college degree will make 78% more than someone without a degree! When you factor in that costs to attend college continue to skyrocket, it makes it nearly impossible for many people who come from lower income families to close this gap.

Where people work is also having a major impact on social strife in the United States. In the 1990s, companies were growing and they needed more workers. Instead of trying to find more employees in downtown metropolitan areas, new job growth was occurring in the suburbs.[13] There simply did not appear to be any physical room for companies to expand in densely populated downtown areas, so naturally companies moved outside the cities. But starting in 2010 as job requirements shifted and many middle-class suburban workers didn't have the skills required for a transitioning marketplace, companies started to move back to the downtown and densely populated metropolitan areas to find the right people. This created job scarcity for those in the suburbs and an increase in travel expenses for those who now had to go back to the big city to find or maintain their jobs.

Education is not the only contributing factor to wealth accumulation. It's very well-documented that white workers typically have 10 times more money saved for retirement than Black and Hispanic workers. However, the disparity among White workers is even more interesting. Nearly half of the White population have $5000 or less in savings and therefore are relying completely on Social Security for retirement. Thus it would seem that lower class Whites and average Blacks and Hispanics are all competing for the same piece of the pie.

So you might be asking, "what does all this have to do with people refusing to change?"

The answer is simple.

Human beings will naturally create tribal sub-groups, and it's very well documented that separation into tribes will create an "us vs them" culture over time. It's almost in our DNA for us to find someone to identify as our enemies who are causing all of our problems. Considering how many Americans are faced with despair and hopelessness regarding the economic situations, it is no wonder that they want to blame others for their problems. No matter what they do, they can never seem to get ahead, so the problem must be someone else. And when you start to place blame on others, you are no longer the problem and therefore you don't need to change. The system, the economy, the politicians, etc. are the ones that need to change. Not you. Not us.

Changes and Fears for White Americans

America is a diverse country, but over the past 30 years, nobody has been hit harder than working-class White Americans. While Latinos, Blacks, and well-educated whites have seen economic growth, working class whites have experienced a significant increase in deaths from suicide, alcoholism, and drug abuse.[14] Whether the difficulties facing this demographic stems from changes in technology, globalization, media portrayal, or a lack of educational opportunities, it is clear that the working-class whites have not adapted well to the new requirements of the job market.

Traditionally, human beings will perpetuate the notion that when one group rises up, another group falls. With working-class

Whites, a sense of "White Rage" emerged as all these other racial and ethnic groups started to come in and "take their jobs".[15] The reality is that the majority of wealth was still concentrated among upper-middle and upper class White Males, but since racial divides and advantages for whites have a long history in the United States, many in the working class found it much easier to place blame on minorities for their struggles. With things like Affirmative Action, working-class whites who might not have had as many of the financial advantages as wealthier whites now see their white-ness as a disadvantage in a society that was already passing them by.

There is no clearer evidence to this mindset of a class of people than the matra "Make America Great Again", which insinuates to an earlier time when life was easier (for the working-class white person). There is definitely anger in the voices of the working-class white American, and that is why you see the desire to "go back" to a time when things were "better and more fair". A time when they could support their family and had a stable job. A time when they had control over their life.

The Psychology Behind Entitlement and the Spoiled American

Entitlement. The word itself will make most Americans cringe. The word has become highly politicized over the past decade. Republicans think that Democrats want "entitlement programs" like welfare and government-sponsored health care. On the other hand, Democrats accuse rich Republicans of feeling entitled to do as they please regardless of who they hurt. And all around there is a belief that white Americans feel entitled to a "white is right" way of running America. In the end, neither side is always right and neither side is always wrong.

But do you think that Americans, as a whole, are entitled?

According to BetterHelp.com, a sense of entitlement is the epitome of the "Me! Me! Me!" attitude, one in which the world is supposed to revolve around a single person and what they want.[16] The individual with a sense of entitlement takes, but they rarely give. They prioritize themselves over others at virtually all times and fancy themselves as superior to others. This can come from parenting that allowed their special child to have whatever they wanted. Or it can also develop in someone who was "wronged" when they were younger and now are using this sense of entitlement to cope with that situation.

Either way, the sources of entitlement do tend to point to the child-raising techniques that many middle and upper class children received in the 1980s, 1990s, and 2000s and which has spread to the Working-Class Whites who have had their social classes displaced with technological and demographic shifts since 1980. It appears that we have a perfect storm for creating Americans who are much more likely to feel "entitled" than in past generations.

Things Americans feel entitled to and their origins

While looking at the research, it is clear that Americans are unique in which things they believe they are entitled to and which they are not. Since many of the people who founded what we now know as the United States of America originated from Europe, where social castes were essentially a part of everyday life for centuries, social mobility was extremely difficult. Therefore the Welfare State was created to essentially help the poor who were incapable of helping themselves.

However, since the US never had a royal family or aristocracy, White Americans were always seen as equals. That was never really the case for people of color, which could be an explanation as to why the concept of the American Dream is so different between White and Non-White Americans. Nonetheless, the early immigrants who came to the US adopted an idea of helping thy neighbor and lending a hand to people in need. Eventually, the welfare state was not as important to early American society simply because Americans prided themselves on their ability to move themselves up the social ladder with hard work and cooperation. To the American mind, contrary to the European mind, poverty was not a lifelong sentence. This led to a belief in American Exceptionalism which is the belief that American way of life was superior to others.[17] Since the United States was founded, Americans believed that freedom, the opportunity to overcome any challenge, and that with hard work you could accomplish more than anywhere else on Earth so therefore America must be superior, right? Furthermore, Americans essentially created two classes of poverty: the deserving poor and the undeserving poor. While the rules of who falls into each category were just as made up as the notion of American Exceptionalism, they were all too real to those that found themselves in the worst group.

For the first 200 years of America's existence, while European nations expanded and grew their entitlement programs for their citizens, the United States went in the opposite direction and perpetuated the idea that the government should stay out of citizens' lives. American society had little sympathy for the poor and struggling and with such a massive middle class poverty was something that most people didn't see and couldn't understand. However, in the 1960s, a major shift began to occur and the United States began to institute and redistribute resources to its lower-class citizens. Today nearly HALF of all American families receive benefits from at least one government assistance program. This is largely due to the elderly, who are now using programs like social security and medicare, so it does not necessarily mean that Americans are lazier. But it does mean that Americans are now more reliant on the government for their survival.

The bottom line is that American society now struggles with the ideas of the "self-made man", American Exceptionalism, the rise of much-needed social programs, and the European welfare state. It is a conflict that divides the country and coincides with a decrease in the American middle-class. The psychological impacts of being on either side of this divide is that everyone now feels a need to cling to their beliefs, leading to more division and less flexibility to change and adapt.

Why Entitlement Leads to Inflexibility and Refusal to Change

This entire chapter has presented case after case as to why so many people in the United States refuse to change and adapt to a new, remote economy. Whether that's a result of humanity's innate desire for the path of least resistance, the "I'm special complex" that was created out of parenting style changes in the 80s and 90s, socioeconomic changes in middle America and American Superiority, or a uniquely entitled culture, the point of identifying these factors is not to demonize these American citizens. The point of all this to help you see how if we don't admit that we have created a problem, then we will never be able to find a solution.

Why is this a problem?

It all comes down to one's ability to adapt and evolve.

As I previously mentioned in this book, Covid-19 accelerated an evolutionary process that started back in the late 1990s with the expansion of the internet, and now the evolution has reached critical mass such that those who are unable to adapt and evolve will no longer be able to survive in our society. With no other place to turn, those in danger of extinction will resort to violence, which we are already starting to witness in the US today.

It is widely documented in relationship studies that those who have high entitlement and feel like they should automatically receive admiration and respect from others end up making very poor relationship partners. In the *Journal of Experimental Psychology*, Moeller, Crocker and Bushman argue that entitled people adopt self-image goals (i.e. goals that aim to construct and defend a positive self-image), which then lead to interpersonal conflict and hostility with others who would threaten that image.[18] Surely we've all known that one person who seems to think the world of themselves and can never play well with others because everyone else is always wrong. Think of someone like Angela from The Office.

Moeller, Crocker, and Bushman even managed to calculate that these individuals with high entitlement and high self-image goals usually end their personal relationships around 10 weeks time. Again, we've all known that one man or woman who is constantly bouncing from relationship to relationship and always finding some fault in the ex that was just inexcusable or what not. In the end, those who are highly entitled and have such high self-image end up promoting MORE interpersonal conflict and MORE interpersonal aggressiveness. Ultimately, these individuals end up being the antagonists for many interpersonal problems.

I've just explained to you the consequences of entitlement on a microlevel, but what about how that influences the macro level of a society?

In today's interconnected world, people are now able to conGaryate and meet in ways that were never available prior to the mid-2000s. With the explosion of social media, entitled individuals of every age group are now able to instantly display their superiority on multiple platforms and engage in cyber battles with anyone who opposes their beliefs. We've seen how polarizing being a member of a political party has become in the United States. There are no rational discussions of people with opposing beliefs. Republicans lash out at Democrats, liberals lash out at conservatives, and they are all saying the same thing: "I am right. You are wrong. My beliefs are more important than yours. Anyone who opposes me is inferior."

It is entitlement at its finest.

The worst part is that it does not take much for these outspoken and ornery few to impact the lives of many. The 2016 Presidential election was essentially determined by 79,316 votes in the states of Pennsylvania, Michigan, and Wisconsin. That percentage of the population (.02% of the US population to be specific) turned the tide in Trump's favor and elected one of the most controversial Presidents that the US has ever known.
Am I saying that all 79,316 of those voters were entitled Americans? Or that all Trump supporters are entitled?

Absolutely not.

What I am saying is that even a small fraction of the American population can make a major impact on how the majority live their lives. This is the reality of the world that we live in today and why we must be so aware of the tiny factions within our society that, over time, can have a major influence on the progress (or decline) of our nation, our economy, and our society as a whole. Now that we know why the refusal of so many to change can impact the global economy, let's now look at ways the early-adopters and the ones who are eager to change can survive and thrive in the most complicated global pandemics in over 100 years.

Chapter 5

The Four Types of Customers in a Crisis.

One time I attended a "Survival Seminar" hosted by this badass named Mike Glover. Mike had built quite a following off the back of his podcast, "Fieldcraft Survival", and while in Los Angeles, a friend of mine mentioned that he was going to see Mike speak. The seminar was billed as a chance to learn survival skills from a former Army Ranger and survival expert. While I'm not averse to roughing it (I love to tent camp...on my air mattress and within walking distance to a flush toilet and shower), I am not by any stretch of the imagination a "survival guy".

I thought to myself that for just $25, I could listen to a real-life commando and learn to overcome any dire situation like building a fire from sticks in the wilderness, diffusing a bomb with a paperclip, and killing zombies with my bare hands. It was a no-brainer so I drove out to for the event.

In the end, the seminar was essentially just three hours of Mike telling war stories and the insane mental and physical challenges he endured through his military training, but there was one nugget of advice that I found astonishing.

Mike said that in any emergency situation, and I mean a situation where people are dying all around, there are essentially 3 types of people. He said that 10% of the population will usually die immediately, meaning that their brains can not mentally handle the stress of the situation and they literally get themselves killed right away. Think of when a building is on fire and these people panic and run INTO the burning building. Yes, those people exist apparently.

The second type of person comprises about 80% of the population. These people have a 50/50 chance of survival based mostly on luck. These people are fairly adaptable and can survive if the conditions are in their favor. However, if the conditions are not in their favor, then they die.

The third type of person, which comprises about 10% of the population, will find a way to survive no matter what. These are the people who will hide under a pile of decaying bodies to avoid capture. They'll cut off arms and legs to escape, crawl over a field of broken glass, and find the will to live through excruciating pain. They have the instinct to survive. True badasses. True warriors.

Whether you agree with Mike Glover or not, what's most fascinating about his story is that, because of Covid-19, American society has been put under immense stress in the midst of which we can see how different people react to the pressure. I agree with many of Mike's points, but I would say there are actually four types of people. I now want to point out the different types of people in relation to business survival that I've personally encountered during this pandemic, and I'll tell you exactly how to handle each of them.

The Rescue Seeker

In the early stages of the pandemic, we saw many people who called the pandemic a "hoax" or seemed to think that this was not really something that was happening. In the business community, you had people who pinned all their hopes and dreams on a government bailout or some magical force that was going to come and save them. I call these people "The Rescue Seekers" because when shit hit the fan, instead of getting into action-mode they decided they would just sit on the sidelines and wait for someone else to save them.

A Rescue Seeker is someone who always wants to "wait it out". You might call them laggards or slow starters. Either way, these folks have a hard time adjusting to any type of change and usually don't have the internal forces to push past their own fears and hesitations.

It's always difficult to see someone you love turn out to be a Rescue Seeker mainly because you know that with just a little hard work and a lot of forward progress, they could easily survive the crisis, but the reality is that you will never be able to save these people because they aren't willing to save themselves.

The Drowner

This next group of people are the most dangerous in my opinion. I call them "Drowners". We've all met people who think that in order to get ahead they have to take advantage of others. Instead of working hard to advance themselves, they are constantly looking to ride others' coattails or exploit others' goodwill, which the Drowner then uses to stay afloat.
These snakes always have a hidden agenda, and what makes them so dangerous is that they always show up with a kind face but have a dagger waiting for you behind their back. One can usually only identify a Drowner after you've been dragged down by a few other Drowners in the past.

An easy way to spot a Drowner in business is that they always seem to have some crisis or major problem in their life and they desperately need your help. However, they never have the money to pay you for your time or, worse yet, they say they will pay you back "from the profits" or are willing to give you some equity in the business later on. For the most part, this is complete bullshit and you need to stay the hell away from these people.

The reason these people manufacture crises is because kind-hearted suckers are always willing to bail them out. The Drowners are so selfish and so self-absorbed that they are willing to drown YOU if it means they can survive for just one more day.

So in the end, stay the fuck away from these vile creatures.

The Proof Seeker

Hopefully you've seen *The Empire Strikes Back* at some point in your life and remember the scene where Master Yoda is trying to teach young Luke Skywalker the ways of the force in the swamps of the Dagobah System. Yoda urges Luke to use his powers and raise his X-Wing out of the swamp, and after only seconds of trying, Luke gives up and simultaneously loses faith in "The Force". In a short lecture, little Yoda calls Luke out on his bad attitude and magically lifts the X-Wing out of the swamp himself. Luke stands there amazed and decides to devote his life to trying again, learning the ways of The Force and doing anything that Master Yoda tells him to do.

Obviously, you can tell now how much I love Star Wars, but this proves a valuable lesson in business and brings us to our next type of person that I call "The Proof Seeker".

Proof Seekers are interesting creatures, because like Luke Skywalker, they contain lots of talent and skill, but they need a guide that they believe can take them to the next level. A Proof Seeker has spent years building a stable business, and during a crisis, they are worried but not in distress. The Proof Seeker wants to grow and gain the skills to survive and thrive, but they don't know who to follow or what advice to listen to.

With the Proof Seeker, the biggest obstacle to their success is themselves. However, when the right mentor shows them the way and the Proof Seeker sees that results are within their reach, the Proof Seeker will go all-in and win. Proof Seekers are great because they are stable and have a solid foundation to build off, and even though they can be stubborn, they can also be highly successful in a time of crisis.

When we are looking for people to do business with, we love working with Proof Seekers because they don't make rash decisions, are usually pretty disciplined, take action once they have bought in, and are generally very loyal.

The Hungry

It drives me insane when people say that the "economy is closed" or that "nobody is spending money". Complete and total bullshit.

Did you know that right this very second, as you're reading these exact words, your ideal customer is out there researching how to get what you offer? And they are willing to pay top-dollar to get it too!

Never listen to anyone who tells you that money isn't flowing. Money is like "The Force". It surrounds us and binds us all together. This next type of person, The Hungry, understands this fact and helps drive the economy in any situation.

The Hungry have a stable business and income/revenue, which puts them at a huge advantage. They have done the heavy lifting and either anticipated the crisis or have adapted so quickly that they are now growing while others are suffering.

One thing I love about the Hungry, is that they are constantly seeing the opportunities in the world. While most people are blinded by the obstacles, the Hungry are able to read between the lines and see how to make massive profits or gains no matter what. Which is why I tell you that right now, there is a Hungry lead out there who is looking for exactly what you offer. They just need to find you.

Even though there is widespread fear and instability in the global economy, there are thousands of Hungry people out there who have money and are willing to invest it if they have the right guide. They don't just want Yoda, they want Yoda, Obi Wan, Luke Skywalker, Han Solo, Princess Leia, and even Chewbacca. They want it all and will work hard to get it.

The Hungry know that the right people and the right processes can help them to be massively successful because that has been what's helped them in the past. And unlike the Drowner, the Hungry are willing to invest whatever it takes into the right team.

So in conclusion, do whatever you can to attract and deliver to the Hungry! They have the power to change your life if you can change theirs!

PART II
TIME TO CHANGE YOUR PANTS

Chapter 6

The Dangers of the Language

In 2003, I took a Sociology class at the University of California, Santa Barbara. While most of my other classes were lectures held in massive halls with hundreds of students, this course only had about 24 people that met once a week. It was unique by all UCSB standards, but it is one of my favorite college education experiences.

In this class, we had one project that would span the entire 10 weeks. The professor broke up the students into 2 groups of 12 people. Twelve of my classmates would be the "test subjects" and the other 12 would be the observers. At the beginning of the semester, the professor recorded the test subjects talking for 4 hours straight. No prompts or guidance. The test subjects just talked amongst themselves for 4 straight hours and the entire scene was recorded on camera. Nobody even knew what the purpose of this was until after the entire thing had been recorded.

In the next class after the recording session, the professor announced that we would be using the recording for a class project. All of us would be analyzing the human interaction that was captured on the tapes, specifically looking at the communications styles, patterns, social roles, and language that the test subjects used amongst each other. Then you would present your data to the class at the end of the term. It was a fascinating project, and one of the biggest lessons that I learned was the importance of LANGUAGE within a society. The words we use matter, and they matter more than most people recognize. In this chapter I'm going to talk about the language that is often used when referring to the remote economy and how this can determine our success or failure.

The Impact of Language on Behavior

Language can be a very powerful thing. It's not just the words that you use since the language, the structure, and even the past perceptions of that word to different people all play a factor in how your description of the world comes across. Linguistic scholars spend their entire careers looking at the unique features of each language as well as the universal attributes that bind all human language together. Within the past 30 years, sociologists, psychologists, and anthropologists have been able to see how human verbal language was actually created.[19] Through their groundbreaking research, they have uncovered that human language not only gives people a way to communicate, but also shapes the thoughts that citizens have and the socio-economic status and even the way that governments rule.

When it comes to the English language, there are well-documented studies on how sexist terms in the workplace reinforce glass ceilings and make it harder for certain groups to get ahead. For example, a Stanford University study looked at the phrase "Girls are as good as boys at math" and discovered that the structure of that phrase, while well-intended, can actually have a negative impact on both males and females. Instead of encouraging females to see themselves as equals, that one phrase actually has the reverse effect.

It's not actually the words being used but the STRUCTURE of the sentence that makes all the difference. "Girls are as good at boys at math" implies that boys are primarily good at math and that boys have more natural ability at math compared to girls. The Stanford study goes on to prove that if the sentence is written as "Girls and boys are equally as good at math" then it completely changes the perception and thus, removes many inherent biases.[20]

Another example is in languages where there are "masculine" and "feminine" words. In Spanish, the word "bridge" (el puente) is masculine and Spanish-speakers are more likely to describe the bridge as sturdy, towering, dangerous, or strong. On the flip side, in German the word for "bridge" (die brucke) is feminine and therefore Germans are more likely to describe a bridge as being elegant, fragile, beautiful, or slender. Now who is to say which is the correct way of describing a bridge?[21] Afterall, a bridge is an inanimate object that does not have male or female sex organs, but it is fascinating to see how language can create two completely different viewpoints.

Now that you know the impact that language can have on our perception of the world and the people within our world, what do you think are some of the implications of the terms like "virtual assistant" or "virtual employee"?

We've already seen the backlash when the government claims that there are "essential" and "non-essential" employees in the workforce. One could be a University lecturer with a PhD and hundreds of published articles, yet in a split-second, that person is labeled as "non-essential" by the government.

So how do you think "virtual" defines the relationship between employee and employer?
According to the Cambridge Dictionary, the word "virtual" can mean "almost complete". So does that mean that the "virtual" employee is not as "complete" as a full-time, in-office employee?

For many companies, the benefits of hiring virtual staff, virtual assistants, and independent contractors are that they usually avoid some overhead expenses like payroll tax and healthcare benefits. But as we've shown, too often the language can also imply that virtual employees are perceived to be worth LESS than other team members. And when the term "VA" is thrown around so freely, both the employer and employee fall into the trap that one party is essentially disposable.

In the remote economy, we find ourselves in a really peculiar scenario that we have not experienced prior to Covid-19. Nearly everyone is now working virtually. So if everyone is virtual, then is everyone essentially disposable? Companies must now figure out how to manage this culture shift if they are to succeed in this remote economy.

The term "Virtual Assistant" has morphed into a form of propaganda in certain industries in the US, and this propaganda can have many unintended consequences for both the employee and the employer.

In another Stanford study, propaganda in the late 1800s and throughout the mid 1900s had a dramatic impact on stereotypes towards Asians and Asian Americans. For example, in the 1910s, words like "barbaric," "monstrous" and "cruel" were the adjectives most associated with Asian last names. However by the 1990s, Asians and Asian-Americans last names were described as "inhibited," "passive" and "sensitive." This dramatic shift correlates perfectly with the increase of Asian immigrants due to The Immigration and Naturalization Act of 1965 that brought hundreds of thousands of Asian immigrants to the US between 1960-1990. Images of Genghis Khan were then replaced by Long Duk Dong and the demasculinization of Asian and Asian-American men took hold of mainstream media.

Prior to Covid-19, most virtual assistants were seen as being foreigners, and therefore many stereotypes that de-humanized these workers emerged and made it easier to fire them since they were perceived as so "far" away. As we'll see in the next section, the line between "in-house" employee and "virtual" employee are now changed forever and so restructuring your company culture is crucial to surviving this economic shift.

Internal vs External culture

For centuries, you either went to work or you stayed at home. Within the past 15 years, and with the help of internet-based technologies, we have created a work-from-home environment that revolutionized the workforce. Work-from-home no longer means MLMs or envelope stuffing scams. Even doctors can work from home with the help of telemedicine apps.

Prior to Covid-19, only 17% of the workforce worked from home. However the Coronavirus immediately changed that to over 80% according to Liam Martin, CEO and Founder of TimeDoctor.com, a time-tracking software to help with accountability of remote team members and virtual assistants.

While the dynamics of running remotely vs in-office appear to be seamless, we've already established that there are deep culture divides and value imbalances between remote and in-office staff. It appears that the "Us vs Them" mentality has shifted from in-office vs virtual to something new.

"Us vs Them" is nothing out of the ordinary. We've seen more battle lines being drawn in the US in this one decade than in the entire century since the Civil War. According to PsychologyToday.com, there are two main factors that create an "us vs them" environment.[22] The first factor is a perceived competition for resources. If two groups believe that they are in competition for food, shelter, water, or jobs, then it is highly likely that they will see each other as the enemy. For example, in America many low-educated Whites have believed or still believe that immigrants are "stealing their jobs", so in this scenario the competition are immigrants and the thing they are competing for are jobs.

The second thing that creates an "Us vs Them" mentality is self-esteem. Belonging to a group carries a raised sense of self esteem. For instance, if you are a diehard Los Angeles Dodgers fan, you may be critical of the team and the coach, but no matter what, you are still a proud Dodger fan. The membership within the group is tied to your identity and your self-worth. You can criticize the team as part of the group, but an outsider can not. Even if they have the same criticisms that you have, their comments are perceived as an attack against your team, and thus an attack on your self esteem. You will likely get defensive or attack their team back, and thus the conflict ensues.

Since almost all employees are now forced to work remotely, you must proactively ask: how will my team members divide themselves? Will new "us vs them" groups emerge? And if so, who is the "us" and who is the "them"? If you're trying to build any sort of cohesive company culture, then it is CRUCIAL that you eliminate any "Us vs Them" mentalities within the team. Easier said than done of course, but it is definitely easier when you can meet with the suspected parties face-to-face. Ever try to change someone's mind over social media? It's nearly impossible.

As a team leader, it's important that you consider the shift in team dynamics due to remote work and how you can adjust to them so that you maintain a healthy team culture and continue to profit during the quarantined economy.

(We will discuss ways to do this in Chapters 9 and 10)

Infighting and How it Will Kill Your Company Culture

The world is changing every minute, and these massive changes to the workplace and our economy can have drastic negative side effects on your business. I want to now warn you about how these changes to your workforce dynamics and the emergence of "us vs them" groups can be the death of your company culture and your organization.

Many workplace satisfaction studies point that employees today are less happy than their counterparts just two decades earlier. One of the main contributing factors to employee satisfaction is this concept of "Psychological Safety" which in the workplace environment is a fancy way of saying that someone has a feeling of "job security". When employees' psychological safety is high (coupled with a positive company culture), inside-vs-outside groups do not normally occur. However, when psychological safety is low and employees feel that they are competing for scarce resources (i.e. their jobs), then in-vs-outside groups are very likely.[23]

Think about some of the "us vs them" groups that you've probably seen in the workplace. There is "management vs the rest" which is pervasive in many organizations and is institutionalized in most companies that have unions. There are "millenials vs boomers" that you see inside the office but also all over social media and in daily life. Then there is the "IT vs the rest of the employees" as we saw in the old SNL skit *Nick Burns Your Company's Computer Guy* skit played by Jimmy Fallon. Finally, and this is usually a symptom that the company will soon go out of business, is the notion of "company vs customers" where the culture has rotted so badly that the people running the business actually see their customers as the enemy.

Each of these groups are culture killers to any organization. As mentioned, these groups usually sprout up because certain people feel like they are in a competitive battle for resources within the organization and need a group to ally with. Sometimes, there are personality, psychological, or sociological factors that nurture these feelings of distrust, but regardless of the root cause the solution is always the same: identify and eliminate the cause of these cultural cancers.

Take into consideration the massive pressure on our society that we are witnessing with Covid-19. The fact that nobody has a sense of job security plus the threat of death from the virus is pushing all humans to the limit. We are looking at a ticking time bomb.

As leaders, it is imperative that you keep your finger on the pulse of your organization and make sure that in-house staff are not regarding remote staff, VAs, or even contractors as competitors for their jobs. All team members, regardless of how their employment contracts are structured, are on the same team. It does not matter if you work from home, in the office, or in an office halfway around the world, all that matters is the team member's performance, their contributions to the team, and that the company reaches their goals.

Still, sometimes team leaders and management regard their off-site or remote team members as less effective than the in-house staff even when the data says otherwise. Yes, it does require an adjustment to work with remote team members as opposed to sitting next to someone you work with, but with in-house staff, we've seen that employees can actually have worse communication and worse habits due to complacency. This means more inefficiencies and higher labor costs ultimately leading to lost profits for you.

However, profit is not the only thing at stake here. The greater threat is if your remote team members and your in-house staff start to battle with one another, which could cause your entire organization to go under. Remote work is not going away anytime soon so this type of in-fighting could be the kiss of death for your company culture and your company. Workflows and delays between employees could take precedence over serving clients, then client satisfaction plummets, revenues drop, and before you know it the entire company is under water and sinking fast.[24]

In the past, when companies have failed at working with remote staff and in-house staff you can usually trace it back to poor company culture and tribalism between in-house and remote staff. Take what Marissa Mayer, former CEO at Yahoo! did back in 2012 by mandating that all 12,000 of her staff work in the office or quit the company. Mayer, who was secretly appointed as CEO in 2012, had noticed that there were massive problems between their in-office staff versus their remote employees. People on both sides were caught abusing their privileges which negatively impacted productivity and disrupted the company's culture.[25] Mayer attempted to repair the company's culture and usher in a new era of collaboration and innovation. Unfortunately, the damage was already done. Mayer's overnight move to force everyone back to the office immediately backfired because the company culture was already past the point of no return. Her staff soon revolted, she was vilified as the "least" likeable CEO in tech, and she resigned from the company in 2017. Meanwhile, Yahoo! has still not regained any of its former glory. If your efforts for working remotely in the past have failed it's not that your in-house employees are inherently bad or that your remote teams are better, it's that you have not anticipated and eliminated the threat of in-fighting that can come with the territory.

Are you now wondering if your company already has this remote vs in-house virus?

Look at your existing teams and team members and listen to the language that the in-house teams use to describe their remote counterparts. Do you hear language that suggests that the in-house staff don't see their remote counterparts as equals? Do you sense that the in-house team is reluctant to trust their remote team members the same way they do internally? Is there a level of animosity between those who are "stuck" working in the office and those who now "get to work from home"?

If you answered "yes" to any of those questions, then you have a potential crisis on your hands, and with the uncertain health crises in our midst, you need to deal with these issues swiftly and thoroughly.

How to fix the In-house vs Remote Dilemma

We just talked about how an us-vs-them culture can bring down your organization and how you must be able to identify if this plague is infecting your organization between your in-house and remote team members. As we mentioned, not only will these negative sentiments between team members lead to a hostile work environment, but it will erode away at your productivity and eventually eat away at your profits.

Working remotely is inevitable so there is no way to avoid the issue. Instead of accepting that things just won't work as smoothly in a remote work environment, you should look to solve these problems with a systematic approach.

There are two fundamentals in resolving or preventing hostility and tension between your in-house staff and remote team members. By implementing and monitoring these steps, you can very easily restore your company culture, raise productivity, and ensure that your clients are happy and your profits are bountiful.

1) Nurture Psychological Security With All Team Members.

Dividing lines are drawn up when people feel like they are competing for resources. In tumultuous times, in-house staff can often feel resentful or fearful of people that work remotely or are brought in as contractors. Everyone has heard worries like so and so is "taking their job" or that a company "shipped a bunch of jobs overseas". It doesn't matter if that statement is true or not, if your team members believe it to be true, it can insight fear and uncertainty among everyone in the company and battle lines will be drawn to help people guard their resources. In almost every organization that I have seen, there is at least one person on the in-house team that has biases or is reluctant to work with remote team members, and now that the economy has been negatively affected by the Coronavirus a much higher percentage of employees worry that their jobs could be "taken away" and given to someone else.

To improve psychological security with your staff, it is crucial that you communicate clearly with all the team members and let them know the true status of the company. Often as leaders, we feel like we must paint an unrealistic picture of the company's financial outlook to our staff because we fear that if we tell them the truth, our top employees will leave us. Now is not the time to play the role of the overprotective parent. You must be brutally honest with your staff.

If your organization is two months away from closing its doors forever, then it is your duty to tell your staff the magnitude of the situation. If your company is growing profitably and you will be able to hire more team members, regardless of whether they are contractors, remote, or in-house, then you must inform your employees about this positive outlook. It might seem counterintuitive, but communicating to your teams about the good and the bad that your company is facing is the first step to building trust.

Nobody wants to lose their job. Nobody wants to stress out about how they will put food on the table. You can put their minds at ease by letting them know what cards you really have to play. Even if that means that they don't know what their next move should be, you have reduced some of the ambiguity as to the situation. This requires you to swallow your pride as a leader and ask THEM for answers sometimes.

If making use of remote team members, VAs, and contractors means that everyone will get to keep their job for another 3 months, that is better than losing their job tomorrow. If and when you break the news to your staff that you'll now need to introduce remote and contract help, most likely a few of the cancerous people who you've wanted to get rid of anyway will end up leaving your company. This is beneficial two times over because you not only get rid of an asshole within your company, you free up more payroll that can be redistributed to the team members who will help you get through this evolution.

On the contrary, if you do not tell your employees about the financial reality of the company, you risk certain backlash if things do not pan out the way the employees think they should. For example, if you paint a rosy picture of the company's profitability and then you have a couple bad months that lead to layoffs, you will have done irreparable damage with the employees who remain with you. Now the team members have reason to distrust your leadership and will therefore see that they really are fighting for resources. Allies and enemies will be identified, paranoia will set in, and in-fighting is certain to follow. This is how one little mistake can be the downfall of the company and make no mistake, most major business disasters can usually be traced to one key individual making a bad decision.

The solution is ultimately simple. In a crisis, you have to "woman up" and let your troops know exactly where they stand. Honesty will push out the bad eggs, thus freeing up budget for the ones you wish to keep, and it will also let everyone know that if they intend to survive, splintering into us-vs-them groups will only ensure that nobody survives in the end. Have the difficult conversations and you will actually solidify your team members as one unit.

2) Unify everyone under a clear mission

By now everyone in the US (and most people around the globe) have heard the phrase "Make America Great Again". Regardless of whether it makes you cringe or if it inspires hope, there is one thing that is clear: it worked.

The baffling thing about the slogan "Make America Great Again" is that it really doesn't mean anything. When was America great? How will we make it great again? Who is going to make it great? When will it happen?

This super simple slogan does not answer ANY of those questions, but to its target audience, it worked because it was stupidly simple for their target audience to agree with. It's as if the Trump team asked it's tribe:

"Is life great for you now?"

Trumpers: "Nope."

Trump: "Was it great before?"

Trumpers: "Well it was definitely better."

Trump: "Would you like (me) to make life great again for you?"

Trumpers: "YES! Please make it great again!"

Just like that a movement was born that united people all over the US who (on paper) had a multitude of backgrounds, income brackets, and education. There is a huge business lesson for you to learn here about how to unite people. If you want to prevent your company from deteriorating into a cancerous Remote vs In-house staff disaster, then you need to come up with a very simple mission. It can be vague. It can be ambiguous. But it must unite every single member of your organization. They must eat, sleep, and breathe this mantra during every moment they are working for you.

At my company, DUDE®, we know that on the surface we are just another outsourcing company who does web design and development. There are literally thousands of companies out there who look like us on the outside, but on the inside we are so very different. For one, we exclusively work with digital marketing agencies, and we intimately know their pain points when it comes to growing and scaling, which is why we provide them with the people and processes to help take on more projects and scale profitably. We use our talents to find the best human beings who happen to also have great technical skills and provide this human capital to our digital agencies so that they don't have to spend hours searching for them. Plus, we provide standard operating procedures for communication so that projects are done efficiently. And all of our company culture is based on the three principles that we created to keep our clients happy:

- **Bridge**
- **Connect**
- **Deliver**

I must have talked to my team members over 100 times about how we needed to do those three things to keep our clients happy. I gave dozens of examples and essentially campaigned for months using this slogan. I engrained this into the minds of every single team member within our organization to the point that you will never meet someone in our organization who does not know and understand what "Bridge, Connect, and Deliver®" means to our customers and our company.

Why do you need to do this inside of your organization?

It is impossible to have an us vs them battle within your company if all your staff are 100% focused on the same mission.[26] Us vs Them does not work under these conditions as people aren't focusing on themselves or each other. When everyone is trying to put a man on the moon, nobody has time to break the rockets.
This goes back to Leadership 101. A big responsibility of the CEO is to set the vision for the company. You set the course for the ship and let everyone know where they will be going. At the end of the day, remote team members, VAs, contractors, and in-house staff are all going to the same place! You must unite the teams with a slogan, catchphrase, value proposition, mission statement, whatever you want to call it. Something so simple and catchy that people will always remember it and unify around it.

Think about your existing company culture and what inspires your team to be great. If your company is struggling and your people are uninspired, then think back to the early days of the business when things were taking off and everyone was excited at the growth. Go back to your roots and rediscover what made you great in the first place. Figure out what made your company amazing to begin with and make your company great again. Tell the story of your company's future using a mixture of past, present, and future. It sounds too ridiculously simple to be effective, but once you come up with that unifying slogan that brings together your entire organization of in-house and remote and even contractors, then you will see people working efficiently. Barriers will be broken down, the workplace (virtual or in-person) will be fun, and profits will soar.

Chapter 7

Remote Team Members
vs Virtual Assistants

There are still many naysayers out there who want to believe that this work-from-home or remote work environment is just a phase. They think that as soon as the virus goes away, then life will go back to normal. Some even go so far as to believe that the virus will magically disappear and everyone will wake up in a virus-free land. However, I think you know my stance on this by now. If it's not this virus, then it will be the next one, or the next one, or some other catastrophe that keeps our society removed from each other. Whether you like it or not, working and living remotely is here to stay for a very long time.

In this chapter I'm going to discuss some more facts and figures about remote working and what an amazing addition it can be to your business. There are definitely pitfalls that you will need to avoid, but with the proper steps, you can build an incredible business using people from all over the world, all the while becoming more profitable and making everyone in your company happier too.

Why Everyone will be Remote

As much as we all pray and hope that the pandemic will soon be at an end, the data points to a much different reality. Furthermore, there is evidence that this could be the first in a long line of additional pandemics that could further alter our society and the way we interact. I've always taken the approach to prepare for the worst and hope for the best, and even though I consider myself an optimist, I am still preparing for a very challenging time.

The best way to look at what we are enduring today is to view the pandemic as merely an evolution, similarly to thousands of prior evolutions that have advanced our species. Each step furthers the human race and our planet. This situation is no different.

For now, we need to look at a few indicators that will help us to make sense as to why remote work is here to stay and how we must all adapt economically and mentally if we wish our businesses to survive.

In late May 2020, Dr Anthony Fauci proudly predicted that a vaccine for the Coronavirus would be available by the end of the year. As eager as I am to believe his team of researchers and the thousands of brilliant minds that are working to find a cure, there is however another group known as "Superforecasters" who most likely have the correct forecast. Superforecasters are essentially civilian think tanks[27] who collectively try to predict the worlds' events using a mix of scientific methods and intuition.

In the case of the Coronavirus, these superforecasters are predicting that developing a vaccine and the end of this pandemic will last well into 2021. One reason why superforecasters can out-predict scientists and mathematicians is that they bring in different minds and different ways of thinking. Their interdisciplinary approach often helps them solve problems that traditional institutions don't even know exist. For example, while doctors look at the rate at which they are developing vaccine options, superforecasters are looking at data like how many people will wear masks to slow the spread, the belief in conspiracy theories, and the resistance to the vaccine itself.

Finding the right timeline is not about what humans SHOULD do in this emergency situation, but what they will actually do. Humans have proven to be unpredictable creatures, especially considering the mounting psychological issues within American society that we've already observed. When this country is put under stress, the safe bet is that, even though our best and brightest might find a cure by the end of 2020, it will take much longer for it to actually be adopted. This will be yet another case, similarly to the US election of 2016, where a small minority of outliers (which in this case will be the anti-Corona-vaxxers) will change the curve for all of us.

Worst of all, there are many scientists who predict that this could be the first in a long line of pandemics that threaten more lockdowns, more instability, and more deaths. The truth is that the next pandemic is already circulating through our population.[28] While Covid-19 seems to have uniquely emerged and spread throughout the world in weeks, oftentimes pandemics take decades before they reach a global scale. Take for example HIV and AIDS. It took nearly a century before the chimpanzee-born virus spread to humans in Africa and then to the rest of the world.

According to most epidemiologists, the issue is not the animals. The issue is humans. With our more connected world and our exploding population, the distance of us to animals that can spread the next pandemic are both literally and figuratively shrinking. We are closer to the animals that can infect us, which increases the likelihood that future pandemics will ravage our society yet again.

Not convinced?

Experts believe that there could be as many as 1.7 MILLION pandemics that already exist in animals and are simply waiting for the next host.[29] Of all the possible sources for the next pandemic virus, rodents which comprise 50% of all land mammals are the first suspect then followed by bats which comprise 25% of all mammals. It is seemingly impossible to outrun these mammals because we would have to distance ourselves from them and frankly that just is not possible given both of our massive populations constantly intersecting.

Why not just shut down all the markets where rodents and bats are sold as food? That is a fantastic place to start, but it still leaves a 25% chance of a pandemic from another animal source. Let's not forget that many scientists today believe that the Spanish Flu actually came from chickens in the Midwestern US. So really, the culprit could be anywhere.

Let us now shift our focus to the economic impact that will surely follow when the pandemic continues for at least the next couple years. One sector that is currently slow to be impacted by the Coronavirus but that many economists are predicting will have a once-in-a-lifetime meltdown, is commercial real estate.[30]

Since 2009, commercial real estate prices have more than doubled throughout the United States. However, throughout the first and second quarters of 2020, companies of all sizes were forced to work remotely, thousands of businesses closed within a few weeks of the lockdown, and millions of people filed for unemployment.[31]

If and when the virus continues to restrain our society and people begin to default on their leases, who will be ready, willing, and able to sign a corporate lease for a building that they can't even use?

Furthermore, the average office rent for a business in the US is 20% of their total revenue. For the companies that are able to survive and operate remotely, reducing or eliminating that 20% expense will not only keep their employees safe, but it could save that company from going under. For the first time in modern history, commercial real estate from Madison Avenue to Main Street USA will be unusable. Businesses will be unable and unwilling to pay, and the foreclosures will devastate the US economy.

Then there is the additional fallout from the elimination of office space: transportation. With no morning and evening commute, new and used car sales, as well as all the maintenance required to keep the car, running will drop. People will be commuting less and so there will be less need for gas. Companies' spending on advertising will shift, and morning radio shows that rely on morning commuters will be decimated due to low listenership.

I know I've mentioned a lot of doom and gloom, but remember that with any evolution there is rebirth and advancement. Many new industries will emerge and companies who are primed to thrive in a quarantined environment will see massive growth. At the core of this evolution is the ability to adapt to a remote work environment that delivers massive customer value and is still profitable.

Bottom line: If your business can survive remotely, you can thrive. If not, you're dead.

Differences between Remote and Virtual

Hopefully by now you are realizing that your in-house operations are going to have to change for both the short and long-term. It's not an easy feat, but the first thing you'll need to adjust is your mindset regarding what has been known as a "virtual" team vs a remote team. The words might sound the same, but they really have some major differences, and by now you already understand the impact that language can have on the way we perceive people, places, and things.

Ever since the internet made it possible for people from all over the world to connect and work together, our society has created an invisible barrier between the value we place on our virtual staff and their in-house counterparts. One might not look any further than the Milgram Experiment from 1963 for a better understanding of how the physical distance between humans can lead to a greater sense of compliance and dehumanization of another individual.[32]

If you're not familiar with the 1963 study, an experiment was conducted with a test subject who was led to believe that they had to give a person an electric shock for providing wrong answers to a test. There was no shock actually being delivered, but the test subject had no idea. With each wrong answer, the voltage would be raised with a recorded reaction of pain that also escalated with each shock. In the end, every single one of the participants administered at least 300 volts of "electricity" to the stranger, and 65% of them gave their answerer 450 volts, which they knew beforehand could very well kill that other person. The most fascinating part of how this relates to this book is that the DISTANCE between the person getting shocked and the person delivering the shock had a significant influence on how the person giving the shock reacted. In summary, the greater the distance, the easier it is to shock the stranger to death.

Think about how that has played into our perception of virtual assistants. These hardworking people, who are for the most part exactly the same in human makeup as their American managers, are so often thought of as disposable, temporary cogs in a machine. I've been in rooms where people will brag about how many "Philippinos" or "Indians" they have. Obviously, I've never witnessed slavery, but I can only imagine that slave owners spoke similarly about their laborers.

Language has meaning, and unfortunately "virtual" has come to mean something far too dangerous to continue using, especially when all of your team members are now virtual. You can not allow the core of your company culture to be subject to the demeaning and dangerous classifications that we have given to people who work far away and that we never see in-person. This is why the language MUST shift for team members, whether they be full-time, part-time, or contractors. Nobody in your company should be called virtual. In fact, remove the word virtual from the office. In its place, you should use the word REMOTE Team Member. A remote team member implies that they just happen to be working in another office, but they are still as much a part of the team as anyone else. Remote team members are capable. Remote team members are great communicators. Remote team members contribute just as much if not more than their in-house counterparts.

Furthermore, we mentioned before about how important it is to remove the us vs them mentality from your company. It might not seem like that big of a deal since everyone is working from home, but when some employees eventually make their way back to the office while others remain at home, you need to have the right culture set up or you could be laying the groundwork for a war. Do not leave this to chance. You must make a conscious and deliberate decision to stop using the word virtual assistant or virtual employee and replace it with a remote team member or something to that effect. Without this preemptive action, it will be nearly impossible to change the culture and prevent the in-fighting that can cripple your organization.

5 Benefits of Remote Team Members

Let's talk about some of the benefits of having remote team members versus having an entirely in-house staff. I'm only going to list out the 5 biggest ones, but the reality is that there are many benefits and they will vary based on the team member and where they are at in their life. I recommend that you conduct a Myers-Briggs Personality Profile, DISC Assessment, or a Psychometric Exam on every single employee so that you can get a true understanding for their personality type and what drives them. Then you can emphasize the unique benefits of remote working for that individual.

1) Cost-Savings:

The bottom line is the bottom line. With a smaller number of employees, you obviously won't need as big an office, and with most companies spending 20% of their revenue on office space, this will be an immediate and massive cost savings.

But it's not just the rent that you will save money on. There are a million other expenses that come with having human beings in the same location. You will save money on the electricity generated from the heating and air conditioning systems to keep all your folks comfortable. Think about all the money you spend on toilet paper,

paper towels, cleaning supplies, not to mention the labor it takes to keep everything clean. All of those little expenses that total up to thousands of dollars a year can be eliminated.

Then there are office repairs that are constantly coming up. The door to the bathroom breaks or a desk needs to be replaced because someone is constantly kicking it while they work. Someone inadvertently drives their car over a sign in the parking lot and that has to be ripped out, reprinted, and re-installed. When you look at all the expenses that go into running a physical office it's pretty disheartening, but luckily it's incredibly easy to fix. Just get rid of the office.

2) More Autonomy for your Staff:
Working from home requires a certain level of trust. You obviously can't monitor your staff while they are in their homes, so while you do open the door for some dishonest behavior, what's more likely to happen is that your employees will feel more empowered because you have trusted them. Now I am not saying that you shouldn't monitor their work or should just let them run around without any level of supervision. What I am definitely saying is that when people are free to be themselves, they will typically perform at their peak state. This means more productivity, more collaboration, happier clients, and higher profits. Just make sure you hire the right people!

3) Easier to Scale:
Read about any tech startup with aggressive growth and you will always hear them talk about the constant search for more office space. It seems like one of the biggest challenges with scaling is where to put all your people. And with most offices requiring 5, 10, or 20 year leases, it is actually a massive problem. Rents are already so high so you don't want to make the wrong choice. If you get an office that's too big, then you're wasting money. Get an office that's too small and you'll just have to spend money to break a lease, rent and renovate the next office, and move again. Furthermore, any

time you have more people, you need more desks, more computers, more lighting, etc, etc, etc.

Let's look at the flip side though. If you have everyone remote, you don't have to worry about the physical space. You could even budget to host elaborate quarterly kick-off meetings at fancy hotels, restaurants, or bars with the money you saved from not having a giant office. Without the burden of finite walls and square footage, you have infinite possibilities for expansion.

4) Find Top Recruits:

Without a doubt, your employees are your most valuable asset to your company. Anyone who has ever hired someone can tell you that finding great people is incredibly difficult. I personally don't think that the "kids" today are any less responsible or entitled than any other generation. I think that people of all ages and generations are incredibly flawed, and we know that most are not fit to work at my company. In fact, for every 42 developers that apply to work at DUDE®, only ONE will get hired. That's a statistic that we take great pride in, and I encourage you to be just as diligent in who you let into your own business.

You must have talented people in your organization if you have any hope of winning. It's a fallacy to think that the team with the best players will always win, but it's really hard to win if you don't have enough of the right players. With a work-from-home option, you automatically open yourself up to a greater talent pool. Right now, there could be an amazing Project Manager in Des Moines, Iowa who would totally transform your company's operations. Or maybe there is an insanely talented developer in Mexico City who doesn't look at your company as a stepping stone, but as THE dream job! The problem is that companies are always searching for the same big fish in the same pond. You can be a much better recruiter and can find the hidden talent when you offer a remote position. They win and you win.

5) Be a More Productive CEO:

How many times a day do you have people within your office trying to get your attention? How many times a day do you have a fire to put out or an unexpected issue to resolve?

Hopefully it's not that many, but the reality is that at least once a week, our days are interrupted because something pops up that requires our attention and because someone can literally stop us in our tracks. It's so easy to get our day derailed, and we get pulled away from what we should really be working on.

Many studies show that trying to get back into the "groove" of what you were doing can take anywhere from 15 minutes to an hour. As CEOs and entrepreneurs, we are all obsessed with trying to get more done in less time. Let's say you could get back an hour a week. What would you do with an extra 52 hours in a year? What more would you be able to accomplish?

That's the reality of when your staff work remote. There are fewer distractions and interruptions that keep you from doing the high-level tasks that you know you should be doing. Not to mention it gives you more time to clear your head and THINK about your next big move with the company.

Don't get me wrong I love my team members and they are the backbone of my organization. I literally couldn't do what I do without them. But I also realize that some of my most productive days are when I'm working from home. I'm willing to bet it's the same for you.

Instead of trying to create the latest and greatest policy or SOP on when to pull in "the boss" to fix a problem, just remove yourself from the equation. Most likely your people will figure that shit out on their own anyway. They might even come up with better solutions than you would have and at the end of the day you'll be happier, too.

5 Downsides of Remote Team Members

1)   Communication

I will be the first to tell you that I love having my team together. Few things make me happier than when I see a group of team members head to a whiteboard to map out and solve a problem as a group. It's the kind of thing that makes me feel like I'm doing a great job as a leader. In most cases when you're in-house, the lines of communication are clear and open. You can walk over to a coworker's desk or reserve the conference room for a quick powwow and voila, problems are solved quickly. You don't have to worry about misinterpreted, passive-aggressive emails when you can just turn to your coworker and ask them point blank what they meant.

Be that as it may, the times have changed, and we don't always have the luxury of having a completely in-house staff. When it comes to working with remote teams (W2 or outsourced), the number one complaint I hear is related to communication. People take too long to respond, people don't confirm that they are working on the problem, teams aren't able to give status updates to the clients, etc, etc, etc. I'm sure that if you've managed a remote team, you also have a list of communication issues that you've experienced working with remote teams.

These are definitely real problems and can negatively impact every single aspect of your company. There is a reason why the communications teams for SEAL units are so important. It's because no matter how good the soldiers are on the ground, the military knows that if they can't communicate efficiently then there are going to be some major problems and unnecessary casualties. While nobody in your office may die, it is possible that some of your profitability might so you should definitely work to create great communication between your staff and your clients if you wish to succeed in a remote environment.

2)   Collaboration

Going back to my example of the team going to the whiteboard to solve problems, there is something to be said about the power of a team that collaborates. Google calls these the "water-cooler moments" and depending on your company culture, they can be extremely helpful when trying to solve big problems. We've all heard the term "two heads are better than one". While it is up for debate as to how broadly you can apply that statement, for the most part having multiple viewpoints and skill sets can definitely help you fix problems faster in most cases.

When you're working remotely, you can never have those "water-cooler moments" because there simply isn't a water cooler and good luck getting people to send a Slack message to the office saying "I'm going to the fridge to get water if anyone wants to chat on Zoom!" That's just unrealistic, impractical, and more of a distraction than anything else.

However without these spontaneous brainstorming sessions, your company could be missing out on the next big breakthrough. Even children need "free play" to unlock their creativity and make true advancements. This is why there is a movement in youth soccer to do away with all the scheduled and regimented practices and give kids time to play, create, and discover on their own. Many sport psychologists and coaches believe that the helicopter parenting style when it comes to athletics is actually destroying children's abilities to solve problems on their own. This could be very true for your adult employees who need those daily mental breaks and collaborations to solve those complex work conundrums.

3) Company Culture

If you are a small office or a solopreneur then the words "company culture" probably won't mean that much to you. They definitely didn't mean that much to me when I was just starting out. But now that I have 50+ team members, I understand that company culture is EVERYTHING.

Company culture is what will make or break your organization, and it will guide the decisions that happen when you aren't around. These decisions will impact your customer satisfaction and the growth of your business. Speaking from first-hand experience, a bad company culture will suck the life out of your business and out of you so much so that you might end up despising the very company that you founded. On the other hand, a great company culture can be one of the most inspiring and uplifting things that you ever do for yourself and for other human beings.

Human beings are social creatures. We formed tribes in our early evolutionary days to help us survive in a very hostile and dangerous world. Connectivity and a sense of belonging are one of the key things that make us human. Millions of dollars are invested every single year by companies who turn to anthropologists, sociologists, and psychologists to help them solve these company culture issues. Yet, very little research has been conducted on how companies build company culture in a remote world, mainly because we've never had to study it before. In fact, I would argue that people assume creating a company culture is impossible in a remote work environment because of the nature of human beings and our desire to socialize in-person.

Either way, you don't have a choice on working remotely and if you don't make moves to help create a positive company culture while your team is working remotely, then you might be disappointed when you see what is created in your absence.

4)   Productivity Management

When the cats are away, the mice will play. Or something like that.

When you bring up productivity management and time tracking, you're likely to get a range of angry responses. Most people will say that if you have to track your people's time then you have the wrong people or that it will hurt morale. I'm not saying that you need to have this negative relationship with your team members and always be on the lookout for how they are going to steal your time and screw you over. However, you absolutely need to find a way to manage their productivity while they are working from home.

If you are not measuring their productivity or their hours on a consistent basis, I can pretty much guarantee that they will not be doing as much work as they did in the office. It's just the nature of humans to find the path of least resistance and usually that means that they will take their foot off the gas pedal if someone is not pushing them to do their best.

If you're reading this and disagreeing with me, it might be in large because you are a Top 5% performer. I bet that if you look back at all the jobs you've had, you were usually in the top 5-10% compared to all the other employees. You have an internal drive to be great, and it comes very naturally to you. You also have a very hard time understanding people who do not have your drive and are comfortable skating through life and being "average".

Here is a newsflash for you: You are different. You are not average.

With this in mind, you need to adjust the lens through which you see the world and understand things from the average human's point of view. The average person will not push him or herself without a little kick in the pants so it's your job to manage the average. If just 20% of your staff don't produce what they are supposed to, then that can mean massive drops in revenue and massive increases in costs of production. So track time and measure productivity religiously or you could find yourself having some big problems with remote team members.

5) Decreased Client Satisfaction

At DUDE® we are obsessed with keeping our clients happy and we have to be because we have a SAAS-based business model, meaning nearly all our revenue is Monthly Recurring Revenue. The number one killer of your MRR is client churn or client cancellations.

Clients are bound to cancel. They go out of business, they retire, or the husband has an affair and the soon-to-be ex-wife takes everything. Shit happens and you will be on the shit end of that stick from time to time. That's what I call "Allowable Churn", and it should be tracked and measured at all times.

The type of churn that you can control is from your dissatisfied customers. Those are clients who signed up with you and had every intention of working with you for the long-term, but you screwed up and let them down so they cancelled and will probably never come back.

The most painful churn happens when the clients cancel within the first 90 days. That is usually when the clients are the most excited but also the most vulnerable so you have to take great care throughout every step of that working relationship to retain them. Do a great job and they will stay with you forever and tell all their friends about you. Do a bad job and they will hate your guts and tell all your friends about you.

We know that when our clients cancel within the first 3 months it's usually for one of these 3 reasons:

1) We didn't communicate with them on a daily basis about the status of their projects.

2) We missed deadlines.

3) We didn't do our weekly calls with our clients so they know we understand their business.

Plain and simple, that is it. If we do those 3 things, they all stick with us and brag to all their friends about how amazing we are. We have processes to ensure that these 3 areas are covered and we have multiple people keeping all our staff accountable. That's why we have such happy clients.

Now here is the big question....do YOU know why your clients cancel and do you have these systems and people in place to ensure maximum client satisfaction?

And can you ensure maximum client satisfaction with staff scattered across the city, state, country, or world?

If you don't have the answer to that question, then you have a potentially fatal problem on your hands. Your staff might be able to haphazardly keep your clients happy by having everyone in the same office because you put out fires as needed, but the remote world is very different. Working remotely will expose the chinks in your armor so if you don't have the proper systems in place, you will see an increase in client dissatisfaction and potentially an increase in client churn. Both of those are very bad.

Chapter 8

How to Succeed in a Remote World

You've just spent the last chapter listening to me list out all the positives and pitfalls for going remote, but now it's time to tell you all about how to really make a remote team work for your business. This is not fluff or theory. These are the three key factors that have helped us to grow our own business, delight our customers, slash our churn rate, and dramatically grow our profitability. And the best part is that you can implement each of these right away and I'm going to tell you exactly how to do it.

In 2019, our company was at a breaking point. We either had to figure out why our clients were leaving us or we would be forced to close our doors forever. While there were dozens of data points to consider, we discovered that there were basically just three things that determined whether our clients were happy and stayed with us or whether they hated our guts and never came back. When we rolled this out to the team and everyone focused on doing these three things for our clients, our entire business changed for the better almost overnight. It was at this point that these three things transformed from just words into a philosophy and a way of running our entire operations department. Now, I share these three magical things with you.

Bridge, Connect, and Deliver®

There are few moments in my professional career that I feel really altered the course of our company and this happens to be one of them. Let's flash back to mid-2019 when DUDE® was coming off our break out year, but somehow we reached a plateau. As quickly as customers were coming in the door, they were heading out just as fast. No matter how hard I tried, we just could not keep our clients and were making all kinds of silly mistakes along the way. What worked for us in 2018 wasn't working anymore, and we had to figure out why FAST.

I sat down and analyzed all the client complaints, the data from our ticketing system, and tried to determine what went wrong and how we could fix these issues on a global level. I came to realize that there were basically three concepts that made or broke the relationship with the clients.

- Bridge
- Connect
- Deliver

If we screwed those up, we would lose the client. If we hit these categories, our clients would stay forever. So what do they mean?

Let's start with "Bridge". When people typically outsource work, they are usually working with someone halfway around the world. There is rarely real-time communication during normal US business hours, and you scarcely ever do live calls with the workers. I like to call this "the gap" because there is a massive space between the client and the service provider. In our technologically obsessed society, we have come to accept that this is just the way things are and should be. We think that email is the same as phone calls and that Slack messages are just as good as scheduled, weekly video calls. Well, they are NOT.

I discovered that the more we communicated in real-time and the more we did live calls with our clients, the happier they were, especially within the first 60 days of the relationship. This was an absolute revelation for me and so simple I nearly smacked myself for not realizing this earlier. When we BRIDGE that gap, we win. When we don't, we lose. Plain as that.

No matter what business you are in, there will be a "gap" between your operations team and your client and it's your job to bridge that gap as quickly as possible. Your clients want and deserve personal and direct communication. They want to be updated with the status of projects and talk to a live human voice regularly. It will make them FEEL more important and that will result in more profit for your business.

The second revelation I had was "Connect". Once the lines of communication were opened and the client knew that they could talk to us whenever they needed, they began to really trust us. Through our communication standards, our clients always knew what was going on with their projects and we started to really understand how the client operated. Projects then started to flow more efficiently and we were able to do even more for our clients, thus improving their ROI with us. Best yet, our clients started to see us as an extension of their own company.

Time and time again, we hear those exact words from our clients. They consistently tell us through testimonials and case studies how their DUDE® team quickly became an extension of their company and that now they could not do business without us. It's one of the best compliments we could receive, especially since it's a goal that we had set out to accomplish from the beginning.

Our clients knew that if they ever had a problem that they could reach out to their DUDE® team and get the support they needed right away. No 24-hour waiting period or some excuse that it's almost 5pm and it would have to wait til the next day. Their DUDE® team knew that they were counting on us and we felt a moral obligation to help them like they were our family.

That is what we mean by CONNECT. Connecting is about truly and genuinely caring for your client and vice versa the clients caring about the people that are serving them. A deep emotional bond can only be forged with time, but once the connection is created, it's real and long-lasting. If you're not connecting with your clients on a deeper, personal level, then you are doing them and yourself a disservice. People are dying for connection these days so go the extra mile and really form bonds of friendship.

And finally there is "Deliver". This is probably the most obvious, but in my industry, it is something that most people take for granted or don't even acknowledge at all. Deliver is straightforward because it just means doing what you say you're going to do. It means hitting deadlines and delivering projects on-time and on-budget. It means being a woman or man of your word. It means honor and accountability.

Delivering is something so crucial and you must not mess it up. If you screw this up, then you won't have a business for very long. No excuses. Get it done like you said you would.

Individually, "Bridge, Connect, and Deliver®" are all very powerful, but collectively and when used intentionally, they make your business UNSTOPPABLE. These three principles are what we live by and not a single competitor on Earth can touch us. The best part is that you can implement these exact things with both your remote and in-house teams so that both groups will produce amazing results.

Daily Deadline Meetings

While Bridge, Connect, and Deliver® is a bit more philosophical, these next few tips are way more practical. We've all heard of the Morning Kickoff Meeting, which mainly consists of everyone standing around while the boss spouts off some HR news and random goals that everyone should pay attention to. Not all are like this, but most are torturous and unnecessary in the way that they are conducted.

From an operations perspective though, these are actually one of the most crucial meetings that you can have. Here's how you should run that meeting. We call it a "Daily Deadline Meeting". Every morning at 8:30am sharp, each team jumps on a zoom call and we review all the projects that we are working on. Every single member of the team is asked, in front of all their peers, if they know the deadline and if they are going to hit that deadline. If they announce that they are going to have problems completing the project or if they are going to miss the deadline, then the team lead and the team member meet afterward to discuss how to fix it.

This does two things. One, it keeps everyone on the team accountable and two, it let's the team leader know the pulse of every project that is happening that day, week, and month. When done correctly, this meeting can be completed in 10 minutes or less and then you have some time leftover to socialize and have a little bit of fun to start the morning.

We do this every single day and I would encourage every single operations team on Earth to do the same thing, especially if you're working remotely. Do this and you'll never miss a deadline again and have happier clients than ever before.

Daily communication/status updates for all new clients.

We purposely maintain a certain level of paranoia in our company in regards to all our new clients who have been with us for 90 days or less. We imagine that each of them could leave us at any moment and place them in what we call our "RedZone". The Redzone is our list of 20% of customers that we feel could leave at any moment and that we need to watch with constant precision so we don't fail them. Yes, it's stressful, but it's also extremely helpful and ensures that nobody falls through the cracks.

We know that all of our new clients are also extremely suspicious of our capabilities. Part of that is because they have been burned by every overseas team before and the other part is the natural psychology of humans. Many documented psychological studies indicate that everyone will get buyer's remorse at some point. It's inevitable and it's something you can't eliminate, but it's definitely something that you can mitigate.

We control this by providing DAILY STATUS UPDATES to all of our new clients who are with us for 60 days or less. This helps to alleviate the anxiety that our clients have about their projects. Every single day we are telling them what was accomplished and that we're on track to hit the deadline. In the rare event that we ran into a snag, which does happen with web development, we're alerting them well ahead of the expected deadline so that they can alert their clients if needed.

This has become one of the little things that has made a huge difference in our new client satisfaction while also establishing trust and strengthening the relationship between the client and their new team. The clients learn that they can count on their team and that they don't have to worry about looking like a fool in front of their customers for not knowing what's going on with a project.

You might be wondering where I got the idea for this since we do web development and design?

One day I was looking at some recent Amazon.com purchases that I had made, and since I have them delivered to my mailbox, I have to make sure I time it perfectly so that I go to the mailbox on the day that all my packages arrive. And then it hit me. Amazon.com is amazingly good at letting their customers know the status of all their deliveries. They actually use my anxiety about the delivery in their favor by providing me daily (sometimes hourly) status updates with all my purchases. They are telling me when it's picked up. They are telling me when it's packed. They are telling me when it's en route. And finally, they are telling me when it's on the way to MEEEEEE. At DUDE®, we basically took those elements of the Amazon.com shipping process and baked it into our web development and design process for our clients.

Now think about how YOU can take those daily status updates (and your client's anxiety about project/product delivery) and use those to your advantage. In what ways can you communicate with your clients proactively to assure them that they are going to get what they paid for? What communication channels can you use to Bridge, Connect, and Deliver® so that your clients trust you to have their back in their time of need?

Daily Status Updates are one of the breakthroughs that we had for our business and if you can implement something similar I promise that your clients will be happier, your remote teams will have a greater sense of purpose, and your company will grow to new heights. Take what I've given to you and implement it NOW. This is not something to sit on. Get it implemented before moving to the next chapter.

Godspeed.

Chapter 9

How to Build Company Culture in a Remote World

Prior to this year, I personally interviewed and met every single person that we had ever hired in the company. I shook their hand and was intimately involved in the hiring process, usually as the one who gave the final say on whether we hired that person or dismissed them. Early in 2020, I decided to remove myself from that process and then within a few months Covid hit. Now we not only have an entire team of remote staff, but we also have team members that I have never met face-to-face. It's a unique feeling to have people on your payroll that you have never met in real life. You see their work, you interact with them frequently, and you feel like you have a working relationship with them, but the reality is that they are really just some stranger over the internet.

One of the reasons why we have such seamless interaction and strong bonds with all of our remote team members is because we focus on building a strong company culture. We only hire people who are attracted to and who fit our company culture, and so even though we've never met so many of our new people, we still feel like we know them. When growing and scaling a company, culture is everything. You must figure out how to build an amazing company culture even if your team members are thousands of miles away, and the best part is that I'm going to show you how.

How to Make 1000 Miles Away Feel Intimate

Now that you've accepted that remote working is here to stay and you understand how to make it work, you need to focus on building an amazing company culture that will help you delight your customers and explode your profitability. You are not just building a team of dispensable virtual assistants who you can discard at any moment. You are building an impenetrable army of highly-skilled team members, who embody your company values and will let nothing stand in the way of exceeding your customers' expectations and delivering an amazing experience all while maintaining company profitability. The difference is that this army will rarely stand side-by-side, shake hands, or give the occasional "high-five" across cubicles. Your army is remote.

So the question then becomes how to recruit, train, and maintain these soldiers of customer care so that they are prepared for anything and maintain the highest levels of morale?

Ultimately, that is the mission you need to be focused on when moving your organization to a remote work environment. You need to figure out how to keep your troops happy, motivated, and continually innovating even though they are accustomed to the in-house camaraderie that drives most human beings. Remember that nature has hardwired folks to want to be together in the real world and so you need to be able to give your people the feelings of interconnectivity that they would find from in-person interaction but now through a remote work environment.

The simple answer is to follow the "Bridge, Connect, and Deliver®" philosophy, but instead of using that approach to keep your customers happy, use it to keep your staff happy. It can be super effective when applied correctly and lets your people know that you value them as much as you value the clients. People over profits.

To bridge the gap with your remote team members, you need to do more than just email or messenger communication. You must have daily live calls with your staff. Every team member needs to feel heard and appreciated every single day. They need to know that there are open lines of communication and that they can speak to their manager in real-time.

The connection piece of the equation takes a bit longer, just like how trust takes longer to build. We recommend that you have weekly check-ins with your team members about their mental health and their overall sense of well-being. I am not advocating that you try to play therapist with your staff, but take time to talk to them on a deeper level. Let them know about the things that are happening in your life or humanize yourself on a level that everyone can relate to. We have a thing called our "Weekly Sandwich Meetings" where every Monday we get on the call and talk about something great that happened the previous week, something that didn't go so well, and end with an uplifting goal that we are striving to achieve in the coming week. I usually share a story about a struggle I've had or something from my personal life that I hope will show my team that, though I feel the same apprehension that they might be feeling by sharing something personal, I am choosing to move boldly into the darkness armed with my determination, my positive attitude, and a solid plan. Obviously I don't connect with everyone, but I still try.

The other thing I do regularly with my staff is that I talk about the importance of mental health and I try to destigmatize talking to others if you're having a difficult time in your life. I even offer to refer my own therapist to any of the team members if they want someone to talk to. I doubt many CEOs talk about the importance of mental health so openly with their teams, but it helps create bonds of trust and also boosts morale when they know that the commander of the ship deals with the same issues they are going through. Nobody gets left behind on my team. I recommend you do the same.

The last part of this equation is delivering the goods. I am constantly exhibiting my self-discipline and my relentless pursuit of my business and personal goals with the team. As a leader, you can not show weakness in terms of your dedication to the mission. Yes, I miss my targets, but I never ever show that my small failures impact my commitment and my tenacity to eventually reaching success. When it comes to boosting morale and maintaining cohesion with a remote team, the goal is not to hit every goal but to show the team that perseverance is the only acceptable way to live. Your losses will actually strengthen the team's morale if they see you rebounding from one loss to the next without losing any enthusiasm. Great leaders never stop and they raise their team's capacity for greatness by setting an example. Make that a part of who you are, and your remote team will go to war with you.

KPIs when Managing a Remote Team

Key Performance Indicators, or KPIs as you may already know, are key metrics that help to measure the performance of your organization. These factors range from number of leads to client churn rate, and all KPIs help you make better decisions. Hopefully you already have KPIs in place that help you run your business effectively, so what I want to talk about are the KPIs that you need to constantly monitor so that your remote team runs efficiently and doesn't jeopardize the relationship that you have with your customers.

As I mentioned several times before, communication with your existing teams is crucial and you should be conducting your Daily Deadline Meetings with all staff each morning. You will definitely want to make sure that everyone attends those meetings. If you experience attendance issues, you know right away that you need to confront that team member and figure out what is going on. Even if they only miss (or are late to) one meeting, truancy without a good reason can reveal a lack of commitment or devotedness.

When it comes to your daily deadline meetings, the main objective is to make sure you are hitting deadlines. Are you hitting all your deadlines? What percentage of the time do you hit the deadline? If you miss a deadline, how many days in advance are you alerting your client that you are going to miss the deadline?

In our organization, we demand that 95% of the time we hit the deadline and 100% of the time if we miss a deadline we give the client at least 24 hours notice that we are going to miss the deadline. With our business, there are constantly unanticipated challenges that pop up that we have to problem solve. Our staff are highly-skilled to begin with, and we also have procedures to help overcome these obstacles so we can still hit our deadline objectives. But even with these in place, stuff comes up. I'm sure the same thing happens in your organization, so you don't have to try and pretend like you are perfect.

At DUDE®, we constantly measure how effective we are at hitting deadlines and use our ticketing system and constant communication with our staff and clients to ensure that we do hit the deadlines. If we have a delay, then we make damn sure that our clients are prepared for it ahead of time. It's surprising how few companies actually measure this considering how much it helps us retain and delight our customers.

The next KPI that you'll want to measure for remote work excellence are the Completion Times for projects. You might be delivering things on time but were the ETAs that you were giving the client sufficient? Does it normally take your team 3 days to deliver something, but because of the workload, your Project Manager told the client it would take 6 days? Clearly that will help your PM show that deadlines are being hit, but the client will be upset because things are taking too long.

It's really important that you measure this as your staff might be so focused on the first KPI (hitting deadlines) that they forget that getting deliverables into the hands of the client in a reasonable timeframe is equally as important. Again, inside our ticketing system we are able to look at the average completion times for all the different types of projects that we have. Now keep in mind that each project will have a bunch of little variations so you will have to look at the numbers with the understanding that there is some margin of error in the data, but this is always better than having no data at all. Ben Horowitze writes in *"The Hard Thing About Hard Things"* that you usually only have about 10% of the information you wish you had when making a difficult decision, so just be happy with what you have and move forward.

When establishing the "Good, Better, and Best" completion times for all your different project types, you will want to consult with your team about what they think are acceptable numbers. Nothing will create a mutiny faster than throwing arbitrary deadlines in their faces that they are likely to perceive as unattainable. This is where you need to get your people together and let them decide what is possible. After that step, it becomes your job and your leadership team's job to hold them accountable to those numbers, and year over year you can make adjustments and improvements. Make no mistake, you should be constantly making improvements on the numbers. To stand still is to fall behind.

Now the last crucial KPI to measure is the NUMBER of deliverables that your clients are getting each month. We live in a society that is all about instant gratification, thus your clients are always looking at the "WHY D FML?"or "What have you done for me lately?" If someone is paying you for something, you absolutely have to deliver. In fact, it's the most obvious and most important aspect of Bridge, Connect, and Deliver®.

Maybe what you deliver is a long-term project. If so, establish what the mini-goals are throughout the project so the customer can see progress and also knows when you are delivering on those smaller milestones. Providing Deliverables to your client matters and the number of deliverables matters both in justifying ROI and in creating customer satisfaction.

In our business, we know that if a client is not requesting a certain number of projects from their team, it is a big red flag, and we immediately reach out to them for a strategy call. The reason we do this is because we know that if we aren't giving them deliverables at least weekly, we have a much higher probability of losing that customer. Think about what deliverables you must deliver to your client on a daily, weekly, monthly basis, and then measure how well you are hitting those target amounts. The quantity of deliverables matter from a psychological standpoint, so the more results you deliver, the more value you are also delivering.

Finally, all of these KPIs need to be reviewed constantly with your remote team members. From management to frontline team members, each person needs to be aware of these 3 KPIs and the ways that they impact the business. Best of all, you can take these metrics and apply them both on a macro and micro level. Each person on the team should know if they are hitting deadlines, if they are completing projects according to the best-practice ETAs, and how many deliverables they are turning out every month. Then you can easily apply them to client satisfaction and client retention. That is why these are three of the most important KPIs to look at with remote team members as they ensure that everyone is happy and doing their best work. On the flip side, if someone is habitually missing the mark, you can figure out why and possibly anticipate whether this team member is going to work out. If they leave, then you aren't caught by surprise, but hopefully you are able to review their performance, turn them around, and get them happy and producing again. Either way, you win.

Best Practices for Maintaining Company Culture

Company culture is hugely important to your success, especially in a remote working environment, but companies struggle with maintaining company culture when people are far away. In this section, I'm going to talk about some simple best practices to help you maintain your company culture based on what has worked for us. You can easily take these recommendations and implement them for yourself.

At our company, we are huge on accountability so tracking those

KPIs is a no-brainer. But what if you find that you are having a hard time keeping everyone accountable to the metrics? It might mean you have a leadership issue. As I learned after we grew past 30 team members, there is only so much that you can adequately keep track of as a CEO. You must have leaders around you that you trust, that believe in your mission, and who can help keep people moving toward the goal. Leaders are not babysitters, naggers, or disciplinarians. Leaders are people who help the team win consistently and motivate those around them to do their best and accomplish the mission.

You should absolutely have a leader on your team who helps with Human Resources and staff development. Since the world is dependent on employees to do the work, it's crucial that you keep this part of the machine running adequately. Interpersonal issues in your workforce can cripple your organization so you need someone on your team who can help avoid any debilitating staff issues by keeping their pulse on the team. However, it's not just the HR Director's job to be in-tuned with the staff. As the leader, you also need to be monitoring and talking to the frontline troops on a regular basis. Make sure that everyone is following your core values and especially that they understand your company's mission.

The next thing to help you maintain company culture in a remote environment is to constantly let your staff know how the clients are doing and solicit feedback as it can help the team build a deeper sense of connection to each client. If you have the right people, then they naturally want their work to contribute to something bigger than themselves. This where you must CONNECT them to how the work they do is fulfilling the big picture goal. Too many companies have layers and layers of bureaucracy, which make it hard for the staff to know how their work is actually impacting the lives of the clients. You can not have a strong company culture unless everyone in your organization is passionate about serving the client's and the company's mission, so make sure that every single team member knows the "big wins" that you were able to pull off on a daily or weekly basis. Do not leave these until the monthly meeting. Make sure that you are relaying this info to the team members every single week.

Finally, one of our best practices in maintaining your company culture is to openly talk about the importance of mental health with your staff. While taboos about mental health are fading, for many people (especially men) talking about how you are feeling and how you are able to cope with stress or anxiety can be thought of as a sign of weakness. If your team members are struggling mentally, it would be extremely difficult for them to perform at their best. If everyone had the flu or a physical illness, they would not be able to work at their full capacity. The same goes for mental illness.

We advise you to talk openly about the importance of managing and acknowledging your mental health when working remotely. You never want someone to feel like they must suffer in silence or feel ashamed that they are having a difficult time working from home. We make it a point at least once or twice a month to talk about mental health. We have referred many of our staff to therapists that the leadership team has used personally or to resources that can help them find their own mental health professionals. If you can afford it, I would also contribute or pay for mental health support to your staff. It's much more cost effective to pay $100 for a therapy session than to have that person underperform or leave unexpectedly.

Red Flags that will Kill Your Culture

Company culture is so unbelievably important to your organization and yet maintaining company culture throughout the pandemic with a remote environment has proven to be very challenging for most businesses. Afterall, how do you build company culture and meaningful relationships with people that you can never see? It defies the very nature of humanity and our need to integrate and socialize. However, there are several warning signs you can look out for on a microlevel that will let you know if your ship is going down or your company culture is failing (or flailing).

Missing deadlines

This is so blatantly obvious that I feel like it might be silly to talk about it again, but if your staff are not delivering on what they promise to give to the clients, then you have some major problems on your hands. There are few things that will crush your business like missing deadlines. It does not matter if it's a small deadline or if it's a big deadline. Every deadline is a promise, and all promises to your customers matter. They matter so much that breaking a promise to a client needs to be addressed immediately.

Oftentimes, I see leaders worry about discipline or confronting staff in a remote environment because they think that the team member might quit or do something destructive. And since everyone is remote, there is an added belief that the leader has less control over the situation. First of all, if you worry that a remote team member will retaliate and try to hurt your business, then you clearly have the wrong team member. But more likely, the missing of deadlines is more of a cry for help than an act of defiance.

At our company, we hire amazing people and empower them to do great things. If your people are missing deadlines, which clearly is the antithesis of doing great things, then it's very likely that you need to further empower them to do better. That can be as simple as asking them if there is anything wrong, running a virtual happy hour, or sending them lunch through UberEats so the two of you can have a virtual lunch together and talk about anything and everything. Human connection and speaking to people's inherent desire to be heard will open up most doors and fix most problems. Do not shy away from the humanity of your role as a leader.

And definitely do NOT brush it under the rug as more of your staff missing deadlines would potentially harm the relationships with your clients. Be a leader and talk to your troops. They will let you know how to fix the problem.

Disappearing staff

Nobody likes meetings and most people don't like Zoom calls. While you think that the powerpoint you spent all night preparing is the digital equivalent to Martin Luther King Jr.'s "I have a dream speech", it's highly likely that at least one person in your organization will fall asleep halfway through your presentation. Don't take it personally. This is just part of the game.

However, even if some of your people are not as engaged as others, you better make sure that everyone is in attendance. Sure, there are times when someone has a doctor's appointment or an emergency with a client, but a major red flag is when someone does not show up for a team meeting and doesn't let you know they will be late or unable to attend. If they do this more than once, it's a sign that something is majorly wrong.

Usually when this happens, it's a sign of defiance. For some reason, that team member feels like they are not being heard or that their feelings are hurt. I probably don't have to tell you this since you've most likely witnessed it before, but people are silly in that they do not always act rationally. Maybe you didn't acknowledge them at a meeting or didn't give them "enough credit" for a major project. The reasons for their anger and hostility are usually silly and irrational, but they are real to them, so you must acknowledge what is going on.

You don't have to bend over backwards and make a big scene, nor do you have to flog the person in public, but you definitely need to address their absence on a personal level and then make a statement to the group of the importance of attending the meetings. If you have a solid team, then they will let the person know that they screwed up and the group will police itself on your behalf. That's when you know you have the right people in the right seats.

People caring more for themselves rather than the clients

Few things drive me crazier than selfishness. It's something that will get you fired at my company, especially if you act in your own self-interest over helping a client. As much as I would love to put someone on the chopping block because they acted like a selfish jerk and potentially hurt the business, sometimes you have to think with a level-head and figure out if this is also the result of someone acting out rather than them being a piece of shit. By no means am I justifying this behavior, but you have to look at what influences might be happening in the team members environment that might be creating a scarcity mindset.

Having lived in Mexico, I know the impacts that poverty and hunger (real hunger like when you haven't eaten in days) can have on someone's actions. During the pandemic, we saw people acting out in really strange ways. For example, take all the idiots who ran out and hoarded toilet paper in the United States (ironically, this did not happen in Mexico which says something about people in the US in my humble opinion). In a pandemic where people are dying from lung and breathing issues, there was a small but mighty part of American society that decided to buy all the paper one uses to wipe their ass as a way to combat the virus. The reality is these people were so desperate for a sense of control that they turned to irrational means to convince themselves they could survive the instability in the world. Unfortunately this is human nature at its worst, but it also reveals human nature at its core.

At the end of the day, when you push anyone far enough, they will resort to fighting for survival and will act like a selfish little monkey toddler. Your remote team member who does something to only benefit herself/himself might be really saying that they are fearful for their survival in both a literal and figurative sense. It's important that you or your staff are in-tune with each team member's mental health and sense of security.

Infighting

We have talked about this before in the section on "us vs them" and the destructive nature that this can have on in-office staff and remote team members, but if you start to see infighting within your remote staff, it can be just as damaging. This is clearly indicative of a virtual power struggle and a scarcity mindset around company resources. They might think that someone is going to steal their job or that because their friend in another company got laid off, they think that your company is also in trouble and therefore they are in danger. Transparency about the resources and the state of the company can easily overcome this.

Never let your troops believe that the world is all sunshine and roses when the reality is things are really difficult. You will only end up hurting yourself in the end when you have to cut 20% of the staff out of nowhere. But also, don't downplay your successes for fear that people are going to ask for raises now that they know that better times lay ahead. With this type of financial transparency you might have some staff that go look for another job if you can't give them the pay increase they want. Oftentimes these people have their own financial difficulties or they are just greedy, and neither of these are within your control. Just expect that to keep some of your best people, you are going to have to let them taste some of the rewards from the company doing well. You should be happy to do this, too.

Don't let your ego or your fear get in the way of communicating clearly to your staff about how the essential resources of the company are doing. If you had a plan to give out bonuses but now have to scrap that to save the company from going under, then you MUST tell them and be direct about it. If you don't know the answer to something, then you have to tell them that you don't know the answer. It doesn't make you a bad leader. Sometimes you just don't have all the information you wish you had, but you are forced to make a life or death decision based on your instinct. That's when the real leaders show what they are made of and find a way to keep the team together despite the possibility of failure.

Forgetting that you serve them

The final culture killer in the remote work environment all comes down to one person: YOU.

When was the last time you really looked at yourself in the mirror and analyzed how good you are at your job and as a leader?

When was the last time something bad happened in the business and instead of blaming others, you simply accepted that you were not good enough and that you did not properly prepare for the challenge?

As the boss, it is far too easy to place the blame on others when things don't go right. I see owners blaming the staff, blaming the economy, blaming the government, blaming the virus, etc. Even if it's just for a split second, placing blame on external factors hurts you more than it helps. The real leaders also look inward and accept the mistakes they made that eventually led or contributed to the failure. Then they get up and start moving forward again with enthusiasm, confidence, and a little more knowledge.

When it comes to building company culture, a fair amount of leaders forget that part of their job is to put people in a position to succeed. They forget that they are there to SERVE and not just to be served. Maybe it's ego or maybe it's incompetence, but far too often the leader of the company destroys their own company's heart and soul by forgetting the importance of their own teammates.

Gain the respect of your staff and instill confidence in them by showing that you will go through hell for them. Always be the one leading the charge. Some people think that leadership is just paying someone to do the crap work that you don't want to do yourself. That is absolute horseshit. Real leadership is showing your team that no matter what the task is, that you'll get down in the mud and do it with them. That no job is beneath you. When you have the right team members around you, they will eagerly jump in the mud with you and go through anything to support you.

You must figure out a way to do this virtually. You must communicate your own challenges and set the example for them. Show that you maintain your focus. Share your fears and disappointments with everyone on your team. Create connections and bridge the gap between your staff and you. This will let them know you are in the same fight together, and you'll be a better leader because of it.

Chapter 10

Deliver Amazing Customer Experiences with Your Remote Team

If you run a successful business then hopefully your customer's satisfaction is at the core of your existence. Most successful businesses put their customers in the number one or two spot on the list of priorities and that's one of the main reasons why they got to be successful in the first place. Customer satisfaction in its highest form is intentional and driven by people creating amazing moments for other people. The question is how do you maintain that when your people are scattered and your customers are fearful or confused or both?

In this chapter, I'm going to discuss how to keep your clients happy, how to keep them referring more of their peers to you, and how you can pinpoint the warning signs that you're about to lose clients even if you are hundreds of miles away from your team members and thousands of miles away from your clients. It's really not that hard if you just know what to look for, which is exactly what I'm going to give you.

Delivering Virtual "Hugs" to your clients.

Whatever your typical communication cadence is with your clients in a face-to-face environment, you need to double or even triple it in a virtual environment. Think about it for a second. How warm and fuzzy does a "virtual hug" or a "hug" emoji make you feel at the end of a hard day? Compare that to a comforting embrace from a parent after you just had your first breakup or the look of pride from your father when you took home that first place trophy? They don't even deserve to be compared in the same sentence, right?

That's because human beings have worked and evolved side-by-side for millenia. Only in the last 15 years has the internet made it possible for commerce and communication to take place virtually. When it comes to your customers, you need to learn how to deliver those "virtual" hugs and break through the mental blocks that prevent humans from feeling that deep-rooted connection through the internet.

The absolute first thing that you need to do is to communicate MORE with your customers, especially during the first few months of the business relationship. We recommend that you communicate with your clients at least once a week in a remote environment. If you can do every single day, then that is even better. I'm not talking about some halfass, template email that your marketing department created and spammed everything with. Each client should already have a dedicated technical AND experience manager that they can reach out to at a moment's notice. The communication you send to your clients on a weekly or daily basis needs to be personal and it needs to be meaningful. Don't think that you have to write a Pulitzer Prize winning email or text message. All you have to do is just let them know that THEIR project is on track to hit the deadline and what stage THEIR project is at.

Email and text is not enough though. You absolutely need to be doing video or at least phone calls with your clients once a week. These go beyond serving your clients. They help deepen the emotional bonds between your client and your team members. Don't forget that your team members need to feel emotionally connected to their work, too. The best way to accomplish that is to make sure that every single person on your team knows the meaning and purpose of serving each customer. You need your team members to be willing to go the extra mile for that customer and I've never met a team member who will do that unless they have an emotional connection to the customer. Live communication on Zoom or by phone is the only way to do that in a remote environment. It's not "scalable" but then neither is telling your kids you love them. It's more important to develop connection and customer "wow" than it is to scale in the remote world.

Next up let's talk about delivering small and big wins throughout the customer's journey. Whether you are providing a one-time service or on-going support, you absolutely should have customer benchmarks along the way. Far too often, people managing big projects never slow down and celebrate the mini-milestones when they're so focused on the end goal of climbing Mount Everest. Conversely, people managing small projects never recognize that all those tiny steps have gotten the customer up and over 3 mountain ranges.

This is why you absolutely need to up your customer experience game and establish benchmarks along the way that you and the client agree upon and then celebrate those milestones when they come up. Fifty percent of the time, our customer experience person is reminding the client of what their goals are and showing them that those goals were attained. You will need to build this into your customer journey as an essential reminder to celebrate those goals.

Big project people need to map out the specific mini-goals within a project, make sure that you deliver and hit those deadlines, and then take a step back and celebrate those accomplishments with the client. As a good rule of thumb, you never want to go longer than 3 weeks without delivering some sort of "win" to the client (ideally 2 weeks or less for a small "win").

For the small project people, you absolutely need to create a packet or a customer "road map" so the client has a constant reminder of where the goal-line is. Small, on-going projects usually get very little love because there is so much going on that it's hard to even remember what was done, let alone what the big picture goal was. That's why your team members need to celebrate the big milestones. Maybe that's for completing 50 tasks, or for helping the client generate $10,000 in revenue, or even if it's just that the client has been with you for a year. All of those things need to be celebrated with the client to deliver that virtual bear hug, show that you care, and that you're doing your job.

One of the big questions I get from people in regards to Customer Experience is how to budget for it. It's pretty simple actually. You just put it in the budget. Seriously. It's shocking when I hear people telling me that they can't afford to do any customer thank you gifts, and then I ask to see their budget and they don't have one. You don't have to spend a ton of money to make someone's day. I'll bet that some of the most thoughtful and tear-jerking presents you ever received during your life were handmade so don't go telling me you don't have it in the budget.

However, if you have the CFO breathing down your neck every month on how to budget for it, then here is a simple formula for client rewards gifts:

- Immediately Upon Sign Up Gift: 8% of Month 1 Profit
- 6 month Anniversary Gift: 5% of Month 6 Profit
- 1 Year Anniversary Gift: 7% of Month 12 Profit
- 2 Year Anniversary Gift: 25% of Month 24 Profit

That is the bare-minimum in my opinion of what you can do to really wow your clients while also keeping things within your budget. Now that you have the percentage, put your thinking caps on and come up with some really kickass gifts to send to your clients to let them know you care. They should open the box and not only be happy with what's inside but be moved by the thought and affection that went into their special gifts. It's incredibly easy and fun when you do it right, and it can also lead to the next thing that I want to talk about.

Now that you've successfully delivered a bunch of virtual hugs to your clients and have a staff who are super engaged and love your customers, it's time to use that amazing customer experience to help you get more clients. I bet if you surveyed 100 companies, only one would say that they are really using Client Case Studies to help attract new customers. It's one of the most overlooked tools in your marketing arsenal, yet one of the most cost-effective and rewarding if done right.

Now, I might classify Client Case Studies a bit differently than a lot of other people do, but to me a client case study is just a fancy way of saying "testimonial". This is a little known fact actually: clients HATE the word testimonial. For some reason, giving a testimonial has come to mean this super awkward uncomfortable speech that the customer is forced to give and puts a ton of pressure on them. On the other hand, INTERVIEWING a happy client for a Case Study is a totally non-threatening scientific study that will help to further the progress of humankind. It sounds ridiculous, but I can tell you with 100% certainty that if you use the word testimonial, you'll hear crickets, while if you ask the client to be interviewed for a case study, you will have more volunteers than you know what to do with.

You now need to schedule it into your customer journey that between day 60 and 100 you ask your happy customers if you can interview them for a case study. Tell them that it's just a quick 10-15 minute interview and that you want to share their success story with other people so that you can hopefully attract 100 other clients just like them. It will work every single time and you'll have such a huge database of Zoom client testimonials to leverage for retargeting campaigns, social media, and definitely on your website.

***It is important to note that when you ask them for the Case Study, you might be tempted to try and pay them or financially reward them for their time. That is a huge "no-no". You want it to seem authentic, and by offering to pay that person, it taints the good deed that they are trying to do for you.

How most companies get it "wrong"

As with most things in life, there is definitely a "wrong" way to create an amazing customer experience in a remote environment. I actually mentioned one of them in the last section just now about paying your clients for their case study interviews. I'm going to spend a little time talking about the "don'ts" when it comes to making people feel special in a remote working environment.

The first thing is that you absolutely do not want to force my company culture or anyone else's company culture down your client's throat. You are definitely not me. For example, in 2018 I put all our cash on the line and invested in a conference to help grow DUDE®. I was determined to do anything to make this conference a success, and so I decided to dress up in a custom Mexican wrestler costume to try and capture attention at our booth. Most likely you have never walked around a tradeshow floor in a spandex Mexican wrestler suit. If that's not your style, then don't try to copy me or anyone else's crazy stuff. Be your authentic self. and it's important that your company is its authentic self, too. In this instance, mimicry is not the highest form of flattery. It just makes you look lame. So come up with your own ideas and don't try to force something that isn't your brand or company culture.

The next thing that I see companies doing wrong when it comes to making their clients feel amazing is that they don't have the right team members in the first place. This is especially true in tech industries who put an overwhelming emphasis on the technical skills of an employee over the soft skills. We at DUDE® always, always, always hire for soft skills first, which makes it a lot easier when we're trying to get the team fired up on new ways to delight our customers.

Unfortunately, if you have the wrong people who do not care about the client's well-being and all these employees want to do is sit at their desk and bang away at spreadsheets, then you will never be able to build a company culture that can truly knock it out of the park for your customer. You simply have too many of the wrong people, and you need to find the right ones. This is actually one of the biggest challenges that technology companies face right now. Don't get me wrong, you absolutely need technical skills, but if you want to grow an amazing company culture then you need the soft skills paired with the technical skills. Tragically, many of the super high-tech companies can't even find the people with the technical skills, so they are having to fly them in from all over the world and/ or they are completely ignoring the importance of soft skills because their short-term win is more important than their long-term.

It's a really sad game that you must not get yourself wrapped up into. You must find great, empathetic human beings who happen to also have the technical skill that you need. Those people have the DNA for true innovation because they will put it all on the line for your company but also be able to put themselves inside the customers' shoes so they can solve real problems. They are also the ones who will completely buy into the crazy customer experience stuff that you are wanting to implement for your customers. Maybe, they'll even walk alongside you at the industry trade show in a spandex Mexican wrestler costume to get a few laughs and take a few pictures with your customers.

In all seriousness, I do want to segue back into the Mexican wrestling costume thing. I did that because I knew that it would capture attention we sorely needed after spending $10,000.00 on our very first trade show booth. This is when we were only doing $12,000.00 in revenue by the way so I had pretty much everything riding on this event and was willing to do literally anything to make that show a success. By no means did I have any intention or desire to try and become a hit sensation on YouTube. I did it because I knew it would work at the convention and because it also fit in perfectly with our brand and our weird culture.

Too many companies do things for the wrong reasons. They try to go "viral" and it's 100% the wrong motivation when it comes to trying to deliver an amazing customer experience for your clients. Do NOT deliver presents to your clients and guilt them into leaving you a video on social media or something cheesy like that. Those pleas for attention are not going to get popular because it's literally the antithesis of how viral videos work. And on a much more important note, you are delivering a great customer experience because you love the CUSTOMER not because you think it will get you a million likes on Facestergrammertok.

If you <u>happen</u> to go viral, then that's an added benefit. But never should the phrase "we can go viral" ever come up in a meeting around customer experience and how to make your clients feel amazing. Don't do it for the camera or for the likes. Do it because it's the right thing to do. Don't let the bottom-line thinking that has destroyed big corporations destroy the sanctity of your customer experience department. Just focus on doing right by the client and make sure all your staff know it.

Last but not least, I can not stress enough the importance of involving your team in this entire process. Remote team or in-house team, you want everyone whose client will be tickled with delight about the present you're giving them to have a say in what goes out the door. Sure you'll get some weird recommendations that have zero chance of making it to the client, but that's not the point. The point is that everyone gets fired up about sending these presents. At our company, we had our designers do all the logos and graphics that went out, and they were all so excited about the presents that they were requesting some of the swag for themselves. That's the power of involving your team! You can get everyone pumped up about helping the clients and recognizing that you, as a company, go way above and beyond the call of duty for the clients.

I am a strong believer that I suck at many things in this life. While I am passionate about all of my clients and their happiness, I typically suck at displaying that admiration in a way that is generally appreciated by humans. For this exact reason, I lean on my team members to come up with the ideas. Your team members will most likely come up with some amazing ideas that you have never thought of, especially if you have a Customer Experience Director on staff whose main job is to look after the well-being of the clients so that they never leave you. Give your team the reins and they will absolutely blow it out of the water for your clients. And you'll build a happier, more cohesive team in the process.

Managing the "Red Zone"

At the end of March 2020, our company was in a crisis. We had lost 18% of our revenue overnight due to the Covid-19 pandemic. On top of that, we had just bought out a partner and paid him the first installment of his repayment, which pretty much wiped out our coffers. And finally, we were going into the first full month of lockdown and had absolutely no idea what to expect or if any of us would even live through it.

Things were looking pretty grim to say the least, but you know what they say about necessity being the mother of all invention. When things were at their bleakest, that's exactly what we did.

We invented the "Red Zone".

No, not the "Red Zone" when it comes to the NFL. The DUDE® Red Zone is related to our customers, and if you use it, it can save your ass. I'll start off by giving you the backstory.

Since we had lost 18% of our revenue in March, we were forced to look at how many other customers we figured were vulnerable to be shut down in April. We took all the clients who had previous challenges with payment, all the ones who had previously complained about their own revenue, all the new client relationships, and then finally all the clients who we had made mistakes with or didn't have a great relationship with. All those factions we put into a group. When we looked at the numbers, it totalled right around 20% of our total revenue. So we made the difficult decision to scale back our expenses so that IF we lost that 20% in April, we could still be profitable. Considering that we had already lost so much revenue in March, a bad month in April could easily deliver a deathblow to our company. All we could do was hope for the best, but prepare for the worst. We could not afford to screw this up.

While we were crunching numbers, we knew that we could always control how we utilize the "Bridge, Connect, and Deliver®" philosophy regardless of whether we lost one client or all of them. So we shifted our focus to saving as many of those clients in that 20% as we could, and without thinking about it, we called those clients the "Red Zone".

That single move to consciously and strategically track the movement of 20% of our revenue who could potentially cancel has been one of the best decisions we've ever made. We now have specific customers that we watch to make sure are extremely satisfied, and we have a plan in place if they happen to leave. Want to know how well it worked? From the months of April onward, we had a customer churn rate lower than 4%, and in April specifically, we did not lose a single client. Literally, I could not remember the last time we had a 100% retention month. As soon as I saw that, I knew we were on to something big.

The Red Zone for us is one of those magical KPIs that we discovered and that nobody ever talks about. I'm sure this concept is in some fancy pants MBA Program, but as far as I know, this is a certified DUDE® Beast Concept that we created and implemented. I'm going to tell you exactly how we measure the clients that are in our Red Zone and the importance of doing it consistently every single week.

Here are steps we take for the Red Zone clients and how we determine which of them to move into and out of that zone every week. It's a very fluid chart so clients can move in and out of the Red Zone pretty much on a day-by-day basis, and we have weekly calls where we discuss each of these clients and strategize on who to bring in and who to let out of the Red Zone. I'm going to give you our exact Red Zone blueprint so that you can take our expertise and adapt it for your own business.

1. New Clients (60 days or less) - ALL of your clients have buyer's remorse after they sign up with you. You can deny it all you want, but this is a fact. Never, ever take for granted that you need to work to restore their trust starting the second after they sign their contract with you, and don't think that you're guaranteed their payments after the first bill is paid. Keep them in the Red Zone until at least 60 days after they sign up.

2. New and Legacy Clients who miss a pre-scheduled call with their team leader - We have weekly calls with all of our new clients and have found that if the clients miss any or all of their scheduled calls, we are not getting the facetime that we need to Bridge, Connect, and Deliver®. What's the result? Projects take longer to get done, there are more miscommunications and revisions, and we end up having a client who is much more prone to cancel. You must track the number of meetings that your client is cancelling. If a new client misses even one meeting, then you need to escalate efforts and get a Manager involved in the conversation to talk about the importance of the calls and to figure out what is going on. Otherwise you will have those people disappear on you, and you'll be caught unaware. Or you'll identify that this is a client who doesn't communicate well and could be someone you want to drop for the sake of your sanity.

3. Any client whose deadline we missed or they had any negative experience with us - Our company is obsessed with deadlines and oftentimes even more obsessed than our clients. We know that our clients count on us and their clients are counting on them, and we take that commitment really seriously. In the rare case that we do miss a deadline, we automatically put that client on the Red Zone. With

missing deadlines, we know that it's a "3 Strikes and You're Out Rule" meaning that we can probably screw up 3 times in a row before that client drops us. Even when we make it right, we make sure that we do 10 tasks properly without any delays before we take that client out of the red zone. That's a good rule for you guys as well. Make sure you have 10 "good" times to help the client forget about the "bad".

4. Any client who has missed a payment or had trouble with a payment in the last 6 months - As much as we want to be helpful and hopeful for our clients who are struggling, we do need to be realistic and prepare for them missing a payment in the future. If any of your clients have had issues paying bills in the last 6 months, then they need to stay in the Red Zone until their business picks up and they have not had any issues making payments. Since we constantly communicate with our clients, they are happy to share when their business is accelerating, not to mention that we can see how many more requests they send to us.

5. Any client who we believe to have financial difficulties in their business - Our team leaders have great relationships with the clients, and our Customer Experience Department provides another layer of support so that our clients are always taken care of. This leads to the clients being very forthcoming on the state of their business. We love this type of relationship because at the end of the day we really do have our clients' backs. But an ancillary benefit is that clients will tell us when they are having some difficult times and then we know to add that client to the Red Zone. These are some of the easiest to bring out of the Red Zone if we catch them early enough too. They usually need one or two coaching calls to bring them out of their "funk" and then away they go.

6. Any client who has not submitted a request to your team in over two weeks - You might think that a client who isn't using you is still super happy since the bills are being paid. WRONG.

A client who isn't using you either sees you as someone they don't need (and might need to cut) or someone whose work is worth so little that it's easier to just pay the bill then have to deal with your annoying face. Client engagement matters so you want to make sure that your clients are utilizing your services. We are reporting on anyone who hasn't submitted a project in a week and escalating their zone status if we have not received anything in two weeks or more. Usually, we'll schedule a call with the client to talk about what is going on which most of the time turns into a client education call, where we outline how we can best serve them or meet needs that they didn't previously know we could, to get them back on track. This is one of the silent killers. If you don't manage the un-engaged clients, you will lose them at the worst possible time when you could have easily prevented the cancellation altogether.

So now that you know all the little details for our Red Zone qualifications, it's your turn to create your own "Red Zone" list. Don't just add customers to it, but actually look at the data, talk to your team members, and create a systematic method for measuring this crucial KPI. And when it comes to clients that are placed on the Red Zone list, just remember to treat them with the same extra special care you give all your clients while still recognizing that somewhere along the line you guys lost your way and now you need to find it again. You don't have to brand these fine folks with a Scarlet Letter and I would never tell them that they are on your Red Zone list, but keep an eye out.

The Red Zone has been absolutely crucial in maximizing our retention, keeping our clients happier, and maximizing our profit. I may not be an economics professor, but I know that keeping good and highly-profitable clients for a longer time period is absolutely essential to running a successful business. Design your Red Zone and use your team to manage it, and you'll have one of the most profitable tools in your entire arsenal.

How to Get Remote Team Members to Obsess About Clients They Will Never Meet

I've just given you the "skeleton" for creating an amazing customer experience that your clients will rave about to all their friends. Now, I want to take some time in the final part of this chapter to really tie in all the little details that your remote team will need to deliver on. There are a ton of little particulars that you'll need to iron out if you really want to blow your clients away. Here is what has worked specifically for us, and by sharing this, hopefully you'll be able to take some of our process and use them for yourself.

To get started, at the core of what makes an amazing customer experience for remote teams is having amazing team members who embrace 100% of the Bridge, Connect, and Deliver® principles. That is an absolute must. If you can't get your team fired up about that, then you're on an uphill battle. However for the sake of our explanation, let's just assume that your team is already onboard with Bridge, Connect, and Deliver®, and move on to the next phase.

There are two major mistakes that people make after they get a signed contract back from a client. They either wait too long to onboard their clients or they are completely winging it when it comes to the new customer journey... or both. You want to get your customers onboarded as fast as possible using live communication. You need them to be talking in real-time with their new team leader very soon after they sign up with you. I highly recommend that you script out this journey as accurately as humanly possible. Every remote team member needs to see how they fit into the bigger picture and they need to understand the importance that they have in this giant machine you're building.

One of my favorite stories that I ever heard was of when John F

Kennedy was leading the charge to put a man on the moon before the Russians did. The Americans had been getting their butts kicked by the Russians throughout the entire space race, so putting a man on the moon became an obsession for Kennedy. While touring NASA, John F. Kennedy ran into a janitor who was mopping the floors of the facility. President Kennedy introduced himself and asked the man what he did at NASA? The man, much to the surprise of JFK, responded, "I'm helping to put a man on the moon." This is one of my favorite stories not because of the surprising answer that the janitor provided, but because it exemplifies the type of dedication to the mission that every leader aspires to instill in every individual working on a project. Think about how amazingly efficient and FUN it would be to work around people like that janitor? Those people that put their all into even the smallest task because they know that it's contributing to something bigger. That type of energy and enthusiasm is infectious. With that type of attitude, it's no wonder the Americans were the first to put a man on the moon.

This is exactly the type of passion that you want to infuse in your remote team members. They all have to understand the mission and be 100% committed to helping your customers have the best experience of their lives. Nothing should be left to chance. Every step of their journey should be orchestrated and planned out with precision. Sure there are times when things won't go according to plan, but that's ok. You just get the train back on the tracks and keep on chugging along. Pinpoint the destination and then allow your team to help you map out the journey to it.

By all means, you need to let your remote team members know when things are working and when things are not. We make it a habit to let the entire team know when we have a new client Case Study video launched or when a client gives us some words of gratitude. We also make sure to acknowledge the team leader, the team, and the specific team member(s) who helped make the client's project a success. A little recognition goes a long way, and it motivates the rest of the team to continue striving to do their best.

These team acknowledgements and recognition ceremonies are totally random too. For the most part, the staff never know when or who will be recognized, which always makes it a surprise. One of the things that I hate, and which I think ends up backfiring in the end, is the "Employee of the Month" nonsense. We all know how it goes. Basically, you just pass the baton every month to a different person. Each time you give the trophy out, the person on the receiving end is less and less deserving until you have gone through everyone on the team. By the time you finally get to the weak link on your team, even he knows that he doesn't deserve an award, but you give it to him anyway. Congratulations, you now have a completely meaningless award and you've managed to hurt the self esteem of every team member in the process. Do. Not. Ever. Do. This.

Praise works at our company because it's out of the blue. It's never forced and is always genuine, which is why it matters. Just like you can't force a video to go viral, you can't force a team member to earn recognition. They have to earn it through blood, sweat, and tears so that when the accolades are finally bestowed upon the person, they are appreciative and deserving. If you can do the same for your staff, then you'll have a rockstar team doing rockstar shit for your company because it's now in the DNA of your organization.

PART III
DITCH YOUR PANTS

Chapter 11

The New Customer Experience

Up to this point we have given you access to the Midas Touch when it comes to how to delight your customers and turn them into lifelong, raving fans with the help of your remote team. However, there is no time more crucial in your business relationship with your clients than in the first 60 days. Sure some people will say that the first 100 are really what matters, but in my experience your window of opportunity to turn a person who just gave you money into a recurring client who will tell all their friends about you is really forged within those first 60 days. If you can't blow them away in the first two months, then you'll never keep them. I've seen them this over and over again, which is why I'm stressing the importance of that time period to you repeatedly. So in this chapter we're really going to dive deep and discover the who, what, when, how, and why of creating an amazing New Customer Experience with your remote team and in a remote environment.

Why the First 60-days Are So Crucial with Remote Companies

No matter how great of a salesperson you are or how amazing you think your product is, the fact remains that everyone, and I mean everyone, has at least some sense of buyer's remorse after they purchase your product or service. Frustratingly, 99 times out of 100 that buyer's remorse has nothing to do with you but rather some bad experience the customer had long before you came along. Maybe they were previously ripped off by someone who looks and sounds just like you, or maybe their friend told them right after they signed on the dotted line that their "guy" could do it cheaper. Regardless of the reason, this is the reality that we live in, so you have to understand that you are starting your business relationship in the hole and need to be very intentional on how you're going to climb out of it.

Here's the best part of a new business relationship though: The client will never be more excited to talk to you than on the day that they sign up with you. Meaning you can get all the information you need from that person on day one about how to create and customize an amazing experience for them. Your new client onboarding is the perfect opportunity for you to plant seeds of hope within that new customer. You can immediately remind them why they hired you and why nobody else on earth can solve their problem as well as you can.

Now on the flip side of that coin, every day AFTER they sign up with you, they are simultaneously getting less and less excited to talk to you. I'm sure you know what I'm talking about. We all have those experiences where we have to reach out to the client for something a few weeks after we started their project and you can hear their frustrated attitude coming through the phone. Through their passive-aggressive sighs, you can feel them wanting to reach through the phone, shake you, and say "Just finish this damn thing already!"

Trust me when I say we've all been there before, but now you have the power to make sure that you never find yourself in that position again. This is why it is so important to take a proactive approach to your new client onboarding and solidify that relationship early on. You don't get many golden opportunities like you do in the client onboarding process. During that time frame, you can have the client's undivided attention. They are ready, willing, and able to do anything and everything you ask them to do. Make sure you script out that process and get everything you need from that client so you don't have to spend hours chasing them later on and creating countless unnecessary bottlenecks as they lead to delays and unhappy feelings from your client.

If you can't master onboarding, you'll definitely see an increase in your client churn rate. And it's incredibly difficult to scale a business if you can't retain customers. In our company we have a motto that I think you should also adopt yourself... never lose customers!

Client retention is so important. We have multiple people in our organization whose main focus is to ensure that we don't lose customers. If you have any hopes of getting funding, selling your company, or just sleeping better at night, then you better manage your churn number. And there is no better time frame to predict the client's likelihood to stick with you (or to leave you) than within the first 60 days. At DUDE®, we track the progress of our new clients on a weekly basis. We make sure that they make their weekly calls, that we are getting their projects completed quickly, that they are happy with our ticketing system, that they are submitting a proper amount of requests to their team, and the list goes on and on. We know what leads to long-term client success, and if we can crush it in the first 60 days, then we pretty much have them for life. I'm willing to bet that it's the same for you, too.

But what if your project is guaranteed to take years or even decades, and your customer is under contract so they can't leave you? It doesn't really matter. An unsatisfied customer will leave if they want to, contract or not. If they are under contract, then you actually have even more to lose. To me, a signed agreement can be as much of a noose as it is a safety net. Imagine what it would look like on your reputation if they pulled that contract for lack of performance? That would follow your company around for many years to come. My simple solution to this long-term project dilemma is to simply label the first 60-days the "Learning Period", where you are learning about the client and how they operate while simultaneously that client is learning who you are and how best to utilize you. Everyone can appreciate the importance of learning, and it makes you look highly invested in your client's success when you have a built-in customer education period. This is a fantastic way for you to Bridge, Connect, and Deliver® too, so work this in and your clients will be on the track to success no matter how long the commitment.

The 60-Day New Client Journey

One of the reasons I'm so excited about this chapter is that I get to show off my team's genius. In this section, I am going to share with you Erin Rohner's New Custom Journey. Erin is our Customer Experience Director who created an actual template for our New Custom Journey during the first 60 days. Erin and some of our other team members crafted this exact process that has resulted in massive client satisfaction and more net profit growth than ever before. Below I'll break down the different steps, why we do each, and the impact that it's had on our business.

DAY 1 Welcome to DUDE® email (automated email), schedule for a LIVE onboarding call, give clients access to trainings

As soon as our clients pay, we are immediately welcoming them to our family, sending them an email to schedule for a live one-on-one onboarding call with us, and providing them some key online training resources so that we can begin the education process of how best to work with us with a solid foundation. With the training, we are not trying to supplement the live onboarding with these videos, moreover we are trying to teach our clients the philosophies behind what we believe and our best practices to show how they can better utilize our services. Keep in mind that your client will never be more excited to talk to you or do what you tell them than the day they sign up, so take advantage of their enthusiasm and begin the indoctrination period immediately.

DAY 1 Send Welcome Gift Box

This is one of the things that really makes people uneasy, especially if you offer a money back guarantee. We made the decision to immediately ship out a welcome box, and a badass welcome box at that, to our clients. Even though we offer a 14-day money back guarantee on our services, we made the decision that we would rather capitalize on the opportunity to really "wow" our new customer and get her/him to be so excited about this relationship instead of worry about losing $100 on a welcome box that we might not make our money back on. If you really do a great job for your clients, then there is no better time to make this first impression than by sending an unexpected "shock and awe" box to that person.

DAY 2 Live Onboarding Call

Never, ever, ever try to do a new client onboarding through an online form or Google Document. It's one of the worst things you could possibly do from a Customer Experience Standpoint. In this remote world, you need to be MORE human, and having the first client interaction after the sale take place through a long questionnaire form is really bad. They will never fill out your form correctly, and you will just piss them off. Always do the onboarding with a live person and take the responsibility for doing a lot of work prior to the call off of the clients' shoulders. We always conduct our onboarding call within 24 hours after the client gives us their money because we know that the clock is ticking in terms of how long we have their attention and enthusiasm to follow directions.

DAY 2 Reply from Pod leader and set call appt-

During the live onboarding call, we help the client submit their first request to their team leader. That team leader is immediately replying and also scheduling their first call with the new client. It is extremely important that the team leader replies quickly. After the onboarding call, the client is most likely starting to have their first bout of buyer's remorse. With that in mind, the team leader begins the uphill battle of instilling confidence and building trust with the client. Every email, every call, every slack message matters.

DAY 4 Tips for Success email

By this time, the client has already done their first call with their team leader and probably have gotten their first project completed. The client is hopefully optimistic and is looking forward to the next "test" that they will send to their new team. This is why we send out an email to the clients letting them know some of the best practices that successful clients use to get the most from their team. This also helps to validate the client's optimism with social proof about our service and how it will work for them.

DAY 7 no tickets/check in

At the Day 7 mark, we check our ticketing system to make sure the client has submitted projects to their team leader. Occasionally, we have had some clients not submit a full project to their team. This is a red flag to us because we know that we MUST get them to submit a project to their team or we run the risk of a cancellation. You absolutely need to have engagement with your clients on the service they signed up for. Each day they don't use your service is a day that they are closer to cancelling. Make sure that you are giving them Live Support and a real person to help them adopt your product or else you might have just blown all those Cost of Acquisition dollars for nothing.

DAY 15 Office Hours invite email (automated)

It's surprising how many different forms of communication you need to give your clients. Recently, we set up "Office Hours" so that our clients could jump on a live training each week to learn more about the service, pose questions to our Customer Experience team, and provide feedback on how we can make the service better. Even if nobody uses it, this is still a great tool to show that your company cares about its customers.

DAY 25 Ticket checks, Customer Experience Check-in, and Schedule Month 1 benchmark call

At this point, we are close to completing our first full month of service. More than 99% of the time, if we have completed each of the steps so far including the weekly calls with the clients, then we have an extremely happy client who is on their way to a long-term relationship with us. At this point, we want to ensure the client is happy and double-check that we are accomplishing what we set out to do. Oftentimes, the clients have forgotten what the goal is so we have to remind them of what we initially aimed to do. That not only resets the client's expectations but shows them how invested we are in their success and their progress towards that goal.

DAY 55 Ticket checks, CE Check-in, and Schedule Month 2 benchmark call

Again, we are coming up on the 2-month mark, which for us typically means that we will now have them for life. Your metrics might be different, so it's important that you know where the point is in your customer journey where you know you have a loyal-for-life customer. At this 2-month benchmark, it is extremely important that we review all the things we have accomplished. Often, we will pull reports of all the completed projects as well as their turn-around timelines. In many ways, you are completing a graduation ceremony for the client. By this point, your clients have invested a lot of time in learning and adapting to your processes, and so while they might be super happy with the work you did for them, you also need to reward them for all the "work" they did for you.

DAY 60 Case Study interview request

After the 60-day checkpoint, they should be so happy at how you've improved their life that they are ready to tell everyone they know how great you are. Now is the time to capitalize on that enthusiasm. We schedule the client's case study interview with us, and we also take them off our "Red Zone List" once the case study video is recorded. This is how you turn your client satisfaction system into a lead generation and referral system.

Bonus
DAY 90 CE Check In / 'What to send to DUDE®' coaching call

By the 3-month mark, our clients usually tell us that they feel we are an extension of their digital agency. It is one of the best compliments that we can receive, and it's all part of our master plan, which makes it that much more rewarding. However, our education process has just begun. We will usually schedule a "Coaching Call" with the clients to help them see how we can best help them in the next cycle of working with us. Once you have gained the trust of your clients, you can let them know that they have reached the next "level" and that you want to show them how to get even better results. These coaching sessions also serve as ways to fix any bad behaviors that they might have and deepen the bond you have with them.

Day 120 and Beyond

Our Customer Experience Director is constantly communicating with our clients. On Day 120, we send them a Net Promoter Score survey. On Day 180, we are conducting another live "Check-in" call. On their 6, 12, 18, and 24 month anniversaries, we are sending out more thank-you gifts. And the entire time, we are letting our customers know how much we love them.

This is what most companies fail to do correctly. They fail to let their clients know how much they genuinely care about them. Our customers are not just numbers to us. Our customers are Peggy, John, Chris, Gretchen, Trina, Aaron, Kace, Jake, Cliff, and the list goes on and on. I'm sure there are MBAs that will tell us how we can't scale this or that we are wasting money, but the long-term results that we have accomplished prove our philosophy. Being a great human always makes sense. I hope that this template serves as a foundation for you to build your own New Customer Journey on, and that your own will blow us out of the water. Good luck!

How to Get Clients to Obey the Rules

Clients have a funny way of hiring you to get them new results but wanting you to do things without implementing any new tactics. I don't even think it's a conscious decision, but I would say 99 times out of 100, the scenario comes up where the client will try to undermine the very thing they hired you to do. And unless you have the balls to stand up to them, this can ruin your entire project. So how do you get the clients to obey "the rules" when you are in a remote environment? It's hard enough to get them to follow you when you're face-to-face let alone hundreds or thousands of miles away. But there are a couple secrets that we have learned along the way that I want to share with you now.

Rule #1: Tell them without telling them.

You already know the importance of the onboarding call (and how if you screw that up, your project will go horribly wrong), but there is a Jedi-mind trick that you need to master if you truly want these calls to go smoothly. First off, you must convince your client that you are the absolute expert when it comes to getting them the results they are looking for. The client must believe with 100% certainty that you and only you can help solve their problem. This is accomplished through a combination of conversations in the needs analysis, sales process, and the discovery session(s). Once the client knows that you are God's gift to their business, then you can use this next magical persuasion trick with 100% effectiveness.

During the onboarding call, you will be tasked with asking the client what she or he wants. The reality is that this is just a formality because we already know what the client wants and needs. The reason we ask is to make the client feel like they are a part of the process, but in the end, we will present a solution that we know will work. If the clients really knew what they needed, then they would have implemented it themselves. Clearly they didn't, so they are hiring us for our expertise. However, you can not just jam information down someone's throat. If you try to force feed your client instructions, you'll very likely run into conflict. It's human nature, especially for entrepreneurs, to reject being told what to do. This is why you need to use your Jedi powers and convince them without telling them what to do.

How do you do this?

Ask extremely leading questions. Instead of saying, "Mr. Customer, you must do this if you want xyz results," you need to say: "Mr Customer, based on my years of experience and the fact that you are looking for xyz results and that we've accomplished those exact results for ABC Company using this fancy-pants method, I'm 100% confident that a similar strategy is going to work for you. How does that sound to you?"

Now only an idiot would object to that proposal, especially since you laid the groundwork beforehand for them to believe you are the expert when it comes to their business. In my experience, when you position your "questions" to the client like this, 99.999999% of the time they will take the bait and agree with you. For the .0000001% that disagree, you probably just need to resell them on why they hired you and the big picture goals. But in some instances where that doesn't work, you may actually be better off firing the client. Better to save yourself the pain and agony of dragging them across the finish line and cut them loose now. However, any sane client on earth should listen to you since you've proven to them that this is the most probable way of achieving the desired results.

This isn't the only time you can use this Jedi mind trick either. You can very easily use this same persuasion technique when presenting any solution to your clients to hustle your way to the endzone. This is especially true for marketing agencies who need to present assets and progress as part of the campaign process. When you are presenting your progress to the client, you should let them know how you incorporated their feedback into the deliverable and emphasize why you made the decisions you did based on facts, past results, and the overall mission. By doing those four things, you will have a client eating out of the palm of your hand along with minimal if any revisions. Again, your client would be a fool to not take 100% of your advice given that you are the Jedi Master and can deliver the results that they are looking for.

Rule #2: Identify the Big Picture Goal and How Your System Gets Them There

A major aspect of truly establishing yourself as an expert is understanding the clients' needs even before they tell you what they are. This is one of the reasons why niching down can be so helpful because it gives you industry knowledge to the extent that you know all the challenges of running that type of business. Additionally, it helps you learn the lingo so the clients feel like you're one of them. All this stuff matters when you're trying to establish yourself as the expert. When you've laid that groundwork, it's much easier to establish the Big Picture goal that you're accomplishing for the client. Many times, the client doesn't even know what that big picture goal is so it's your job to identify it for them and hold them accountable to it. For example, the client might think they need a new website, but what they really need is a better Unique Selling Proposition, a solid offer, copy that compels people to buy, a follow-up sequence to nurture leads, a cold-traffic strategy to help them find new prospects, and a way to tie all of this together so they can grow their revenue by 50% month-over-month. If you can pinpoint the big picture even before the client does, you'll have a customer for life.

Clients will almost always lose sight of what that goal is so you will need to constantly remind them of where you are going. That's one of the reasons why our 60-day Customer Journey is so powerful because we systematize the process of reminding a client what our mission objective is. Your client is an extremely busy person and in all likelihood, they have tried to implement your solution multiple times prior to hiring you and have failed every time. It doesn't make sense why they would hire someone only to undermine the objective. But it's human nature to take the path of least resistance, and usually that path is to continue doing things the "old fashioned way".

Not this time though!

By using your Jedi-mind-tricks to get the clients out of their own way, you can alter the course of their business and help them create a new life. However to do this, you must understand that you'll have to help redirect the ship back on track almost daily. Your constant reminders of why they hired you are almost like mini-therapy sessions to help your client develop positive habits that will amount to an amazing new outcome. So do not be discouraged or unprepared for your client forgetting about the big picture or resisting your revolutionary efforts from time to time. Instead, build those reminders about your purpose and all the progress that you're making for them into your processes.

Rule #3: Use Numbers and Facts and Document Everything

This is by far my least favorite aspect of working with clients. In a perfect world, your client would remember all the little moving parts within your project and would never forget to give you the things you need to do your job. They would remember all the things you discussed on calls, they would always reply quickly to emails, and they would always acknowledge the progress that you're making. But we all know that we do not live in a perfect world.

The reality is that your clients will constantly forget what you're doing for them and that it's our job to remove as much responsibility from the client as we can, but even with that said, you must have a process for delivering status updates to your clients. While emotions matter and we always want to make our clients feel like we understand their business better than anyone else, we also need hard facts and data to back us up. You should always have reports with quantifiable data that prove you are getting the results you promised. These reports can be the number of leads, the response times, the revenue numbers, etc. Include whatever you need to prove without a shadow of a doubt that you're making progress and hitting your targets, and present that to the client on a weekly, monthly, and quarterly basis. Keep in mind that in a remote world, you need to be more in their face and communicate even more regularly with your client, so these reports should be presented live and frequently.

The second thing is that you will need to be incredibly meticulous when it comes to documenting the communication with your clients. Doubtless, you'll be conducting a lot of Zoom calls with your clients. Never assume that your clients will remember what you talked about on those calls. In fact, you should assume that the client will forget everything you talked about. Make it a good practice to reply to your client in a message and summarize what was discussed on the call. This might sound like a pain in the ass, and it is, but it will save you tons of anguish later on when you have a discrepancy with a client and you need to find the facts to back up your case.

Now when it comes to documentation, one of the biggest mistakes I see people making is that they rely on email to communicate with their clients. This will absolutely kill you in the long-run. What happens if your team member gets sick and you need to find that email communication they had with your angry client? You can get into their inbox, but what if they deleted the email? You'll be screwed, and most likely it will cost you money and a happy customer. This is why we tell everyone to use a ticketing system like Freshdesk or Zendesk, and possibly a Project Management system with it, so you can very easily track the communication you have with your clients. You'll have easy access no matter which of you is communicating with the client, and it will be incredibly simple to find the messages you need. Trust me and set this up as soon as you finish this chapter. You'll thank me for it later.

Rule #4: Know When to Cut the Client Loose

As Kenny Loggins famously said, you gotta know when to hold 'em, know when to fold 'em, know when to walk away, know when to run.

Same goes for clients. Sometimes you just need to call it quits and chalk it up to a learning experience. In your contracts, you should always have a clause that gives you the right to walk away with or without a refund. Not everyone is going to be a good fit for you and sometimes you figure that out only after you have started working together. It's a good rule of thumb to always listen to your gut. That client you suspect could be a giant PITA (pain in the ass) probably is a giant PITA. Listen to your instincts and avoid the challenging clients before it's too late.

However, sometimes those folks do slide under your radar. You need to have policies in place so that you know exactly when it's time to cut ties and end the relationship. It really does not matter how much they are paying you. If the client is causing you and your staff grief, then you need to let them go. Think about how difficult it is to keep your staff happy and sane in a quarantine environment. You don't want to let one client drive away your people who are literally holding the ship together. Plus, you'll be amazed at how quickly you can replace the revenue from that difficult customer once you've let them go.

If you have taken all the proper steps and your client is still unwilling or unable to get with the program, then you have to go your separate ways. Even if it was a referral or even if it's your best friend's brother. For the sake of your team members, if the client is that big of a disruption, then you need to cut the cord. Most of the time, the client knows that it's not working out too, but if they are the bullying type then they are used to beating down the vendor until they get their way. By no means should you take that kind of abuse. Have some backbone and stand up for yourself, but try to do so without verbally or physically thrashing the client in public. I like to have a list of "friends" that I refer difficult clients to. It's easier to tell the client that you aren't going to be a good fit when you can follow the statement up with the fact that you have someone that you've already spoken to who would be perfect for them. You still come off looking like the good gal/guy, but most importantly you get the problem child off your docket.

The most difficult part of ending the relationship usually comes down to whether or not you have to give a refund. Refunds are especially painful in these situations because for all intents and purposes you did your job and it's the client who couldn't live up to their end of the bargain. You have actual hard costs involved in the project, and those hard costs need to be paid. As much as I love a good fight in real life, when it comes to business, I'll normally refund at least a portion of the fees that have been paid to me. In the end, it saves you time and money as you can just move on with your life. If the client is angrily requesting a refund and you don't give it, you can pretty much guarantee that they will start World War 3 with your company. And in this age of social media, you stand more to lose than he does. Always, always, always jump on a call with the client and talk it out person-to-person. I've had clients demand full refunds, yet after an honest conversation, we are able to part as friends with maybe a couple hundred bucks exchanged instead. Figure out what they really want, offer a little more if needed, and then move on. You'll make the money back in a week.

And those are the 4 tips for how to get your clients to obey the rules. Proper procedures and protocols will go a long way, but never lose sight of the fact that your team member's sanity is also a key reason why you want your clients to stay the course that you laid out for them. And don't be afraid to let the client go if you realize it's not going to be a good fit.

Why You Must Have a Customer Experience Director

One of the best decisions I ever made for our company was to bring on a Customer Experience Director. In 2019, we had a major customer churn issue, and after looking at the numbers, it dawned on me that we lost $1 MILLION because of all our client cancellations. ONE MILLION FUCKING DOLLARS. Now I don't know what kind of financial situation you're in, but from where I come from, a million dollars is a crapload of money. As angry and frustrated as I was, I didn't have anyone to blame but myself. Sure the company had grown astronomically fast and we were forced to invent systems and processes on the fly, but at the end of the day we had lost a ton of customers, and it was all on my watch. I really had no one to blame but myself.

The million dollar question that I had to answer was "How am I going to fix this?"

The reality was that I was failing, not just with our customer churn problem but in multiple areas in the company. I was trying to do too much and I needed leaders who could help to support the massive growth that we had experienced. The skills I learned that helped me run an 8-person company were not the same skills that would help me run a 30-person company. In that moment, I realized that in order for me to solve my customer churn problem, what I really needed was someone who could dramatically improve our customer experience. Customers were signing up with us because they believed in our vision, but we were failing them on the execution.

Not all of the clients were unhappy though. They either loved us and told all their friends about us or they hated us (and also told all their friends). We had to figure out what we were doing right for the first group and what we were doing wrong for the second. And I needed to put someone in charge to help us consistently and predictably get clients to fall in love with us. Admittedly, I suck at customer experience and figuring out the little details of what makes people happy. From a big-picture-standpoint, I am pretty good, but when it comes to the little details that make all the difference, I am the last person you want on that task. However, Erin, our Customer Support Specialist, was absolutely perfect for it.

I met Erin when she and I were working at a newspaper in Los Angeles. She was the Account Manager and Support person for all the digital ad placements, and she was a lifesaver for me. For about 6 months, we would scramble to get ads placed, deal with the creative departments, and wrangle the sales reps so that we could meet our revenue targets. She was the single-most important person in that digital advertising department. So a year after I left the newspaper, I noticed that she had just had her first son. I nonchalantly hit her up on Facebook and asked if she would be interested in some part-time work with my new digital agency. She happily accepted, and in no time, she learned every aspect of the digital agency, eventually taking over as the lead Customer Support Specialist for DUDE®. To this day, our company would not be where we are without her help. She is a one-in-a-million type of team member.

When I realized I need someone to head up a leadership role on the customer experience side, there was literally no better person for the job. Thankfully, she accepted and has helped us take our churn percentage from 16% to 10% to 8% to 4% and finally down to 2.7%. All of this in under 9 months!!!

Obviously, you can't have Erin, but the purpose of me telling you this story is so you can find your OWN Erin. I don't think most agencies have a Customer Experience Director, yet it is one of the single most-important roles you can have within your company, especially if you rely on monthly recurring revenue. In short, a Customer Experience Director is in charge of one thing: Reducing churn so customers stay forever.

You will never grow your company if you don't keep your customers. If your business is a SAAS-based model and you live on monthly recurring revenue, then you MUST have a Customer Experience Director on your payroll to help you stay in touch with your clients, keep them happy, and convince them to never leave you. In this section, I'm going to show you exactly why you need a Customer Experience Director, how to find one even if you don't have a big budget, what they will do for your company, and where to get one in 60 days or less.

What does a Customer Experience Director Do

I'm sure there are dozens of explanations as to what a Customer Experience Director does and what they are supposed to be responsible for, but I'm going to break it down into the simplest explanation possible:

A Customer Experience Director keeps customer churn down as low as humanly possible to increase profitability.

If you run a SAAS-based model and customer retention is crucial for your profitability, then this is the single most important thing that your Customer Experience Director is responsible for. They keep clients happy so they don't cancel. Period. End of story. The methods used for this are infinite, but the mission is always the same.

By now you should have an estimate as to what kind of churn is acceptable in your industry. Don't ever think that you can maintain 100% customer retention forever. Eventually, some of your clients will cancel regardless of whether you provide the best service known to man. The main reason why clients cancel with us is that they just go out of business, so we factor that into our maximum allowable churn rate. It's important that you give yourself an amount for churn that you use as the maximum allowable churn rate per month. Then you simply give your Customer Experience Director the task of keeping the churn rate below that percentage.

How to Find a Customer Experience Director

We are big believers in promoting from within. Erin was our Customer Support Specialist for 5 years prior to taking on this crucial role so she already knew our company culture, how we operated, and all the people she would be managing. It's important that you understand that you are hiring someone whose mind operates like a project manager. You need someone who solves problems and can create solutions as needed. If you hire someone who is constantly waiting for instructions and/or doesn't know how to find solutions to new problems, then you are just going to create more trouble than it is worth. You must hire the right personality first and then the technical skills second.

The beauty of this role is that a Customer Experience Director can live pretty much anywhere, which means that the hiring pool is wide open. It's an ideal role for a digital nomad or stay-at-home-mom who wants a part-time job that also brings a lot of joy to peoples' lives. A happy remote team member who is living out their dream is the perfect candidate for this position, so keep an open mind when looking for this applicant.

Now here is one of the best things that we can provide to you. We will give you the exact job description for our Customer Experience Director position! I'm sure you'll need to change some things up to fit your business' description, but if nothing else, this will give you a guide to use in looking for your own Customer Experience

Director. In the next section, I'll explain in more detail some of the additional things to look out for when hiring your superstar Customer Experience person. So without further ado, here you go:

Customer Experience Director Job Description

We are a web design and web development outsourcing company with the majority of our staff located in Tijuana, B.C. With an efficient and innovative business model, we are looking for an extraordinary person to join and manage our clients to meet and exceed their expectations so that they never cancel our service and tell all their friends about how amazing we are.

You can see more of us in this video: *https://youtu.be/KJ-d2nCx-Jo*

We are looking for an outstanding problem solver who is obsessed with customer service and customer experience and who will support client retention and revenue growth through Customer Experience excellence.

Some of your main responsibilities will be to:

- *Coordinate with the Operations Manager and team leaders to ensure that the operations team are completing projects within an above average timeframe.*
- *Coordinate with the Operations Manager and team leaders so they are responding to clients within an above average timeframe.*
- *Coordinate with the Operations Manager and team leaders, designers, and developers so that every project requested by clients is completed in above average timeframe.*
- *Coordinate with Operations Manager and team leaders to minimize missed client deadlines and ensure client happiness.*
- *Coordinate with Operations Manager and all operations staff to minimize client subscription cancellations.*
- *Coordinate with Operations Manager for the daily communications*

and follow up sent to new clients.
- *Coordinate with Operations Manager and the weekly and monthly communication with new and legacy clients.*
- *Supervise all client Customer Success.*
- *Creating and distributing mass communication to clients such as the monthly Customer Service update, product announcements (collab with Dev team), sale announcements to internal clients (collab with Marketing/Sales).*
- *Supervise the creation, execution, and adjustment of the automated boarding and accolade sequences (email and physical mailing).*
- *Supervise and conduct new client onboarding.*
- *Review collection and response of client feedback and customer satisfaction info.*
- *Case study info: gathering info/interviewing clients (collab with Marketing)*

Provide phone and video call support to clients as needed.
Audit project communication and workflow to maximize efficiency.
Conduct team leader customer experience training, contribute to quarterly company review meetings, and conduct additional customer experience-related meetings as needed.
Problem solve and create solutions and Standard Operating Procedures to improve customer experience for our clients.
Supervise and implement team training for customer experience.
Attend and present at company events and presentations as needed.
Coordinate with the Director of HR and assess monthly and quarterly team leader performance reviews and evaluations.
Must learn something new and teach to a team member each day.
Must read at least one book per quarter related to leadership, customer experience, management or personal development.
Create and distribute client gifts and thank you packages.
Travel to and attendance of seminars and classes may be required for additional learning and training.
Travel to and attendance of conferences may be required for sales and marketing support.

Acknowledge mistakes in the "Growth Book" and help the team to avoid those mistakes in the future.

Be a leader and team player and be willing to sacrifice for the good of your teammates and the company.

Maintain a positive attitude and focus on solutions and not problems.

Maintain a clean workspace and pick up after yourself.

Build daily successful habits and routines to help yourself and your teammates.

Lead by example.

Submit reports on time to the CEO and others on the leadership team.

Report feedback and maintain communication with the CEO

Main soft skill requirements:
> Leadership
> Effective communications skills
> Problem-solving
> Dependability
> Work ethic
> Integrity
> Flexibility
> Decision Making
> Negotiation and conflict resolution
> Organization
> Time management

Hard skills requirements:
> Fluent English (Spanish a bonus)
> Working knowledge of web design and development, digital marketing, project management, and outsourcing
> At least 2 years experience in customer service/customer experience at a digital marketing agency
> At least 2 years supervising a team
> At least 2 years experience working in a digital agency

environment

Experience with Daily, Weekly, Monthly, and Quarterly customer experience goal setting and reporting

Proven track record of meeting customer experience and client retention goals

Experience establishing Standard Operating Procedures

At least 2 Years of Customer Experience/Service

Metrics for Success

1) Delivery of all projects meet company objectives and client expectations

2) Assisting with Quality Control of all Projects

3) Ticketing System function and customer experience

4) Dedicated Employee Production

5) Supervising the creation, execution, and adjustment of client onboarding

6) Client Churn Through Bridge, Connect, and Deliver® Principles

7) Client Referrals and Client Case Studies/Testimonials

8) Churn and Profitability

Requirements, Objectives, and KPIs
Daily Requirements

- Report any major customer experience issues to CEO.
- Maintain monthly customer churn below 8%.
- Maintain Net Promoter Score above 9 out of 10.
- Track all Red Zone clients and report any major Red Zone

issues to CEO.

Weekly Requirements
- Provide Weekly Summary of previous week in regards to Customer Churn and any and all Customer Experience challenges.
- Provide weekly plan to hit monthly objectives and any obstacles to achieving the monthly, quarterly, and yearly goals.
- Attend Pod Leader trainings and provide open dialogue for pod leader growth.
- Spend at least one hour per week with Operations Manager to ensure their success.

Monthly Requirements
- Provide a monthly summary to the CEO with statistics on Customer Churn, NPS, and customer satisfaction. Be prepared to deliver that information to the company and staff.
- Provide a plan for the upcoming month to achieve our monthly, quarterly, and yearly goals broken down by week to week progress.
- Provide recommended improvements/adjustments to help improve the customer experience.
- Work with Finance and Operations teams to ensure that client churn is below 8% per month.

Quarterly Requirements
- Work with the CEO to develop/adjust the quarterly goals based on company yearly objectives.
- Provide guidance and feedback on how to improve the performance of the Customer Experience department.
- Work to improve the ticketing system and client experience to decrease custom churn.

- Recommend suggestions for improving staff performance and growth. Work with HR on recommendations.
- Present Quarterly accomplishments and missteps to company staff at quarterly meetings.

Annual Requirements
- Create a plan to take the CEOs vision and turn that into an annual customer experience plan to achieve company objectives.
- Create a quarterly, monthly, and weekly plan with actionable items to help achieve annual goals.
- Maintain client churn at 8% or less for the year.
- Coordinate with Operations Manager to ensure that average completion times are at adequate levels based on annual revenue, retention, and profit goals.
- Coordinate with Operations Manager to ensure that Dedicated Employee revenue, retention, and profit goals are achieved.
- Coordinate with Operations Manager to create and execute improvements to the Portal Ticketing System to improve customer experience. Work with the Customer Experience team to achieve this goal.
- Work with the Marketing team, Operations Manager and CEO to develop a referral plan for existing customers.

How to Find One and What to Pay

Now that you have the job post for your Customer Experience Director it's time to start looking for her/him. Internal promotions are by far the best, but if that isn't an option then I would look for industry friends who have taken a leave of absence. I have found that it always helps to hire someone who already knows your industry and what customers are looking for. This will save you lots of training when it comes to onboarding your new Customer

Experience Director.

However if you are willing to hire someone from outside your industry, it's crucial to make sure they have lots of experience in Customer Experience. Customer experience is different than customer service in that customer experience is proactive while customer service is reactive. A Customer Experience Director needs to be able to architect how customers interact with your product or service in a way that consistently produces extremely happy clients. This is an art and a skill, but it comes naturally for the right person.

When it comes to what you can pay this person, I believe in a tiered payment plan based on experience and performance. I would start out with this person making a certain salary or hourly rate and then increase it monthly or at the least quarterly based on performance. For example, if your churn percentage is really bad to begin with, give him or her a monthly salary increase for every percentage point that they reduce the rate by. This not only gives your Customer Experience Director incentive to improve your company's retention, but it also allows you to pay them from the increase in profits. Everyone wins.

Think of other things that you can incentivize your Customer Experience Director to help you fix. A very easy way to do this is to look at the job description and identify the KPIs that will really help to move the needle in your company. Retention is clearly the most important KPI, but there are other factors that play into retention too. For instance, improving daily and weekly communication with your clients directly relates to customer satisfaction, so if your Customer Experience Director improves that communication, then that could be another KPI that merits an additional pay incentive. Most likely there are at least five areas you can use to gauge your Customer Experience Director's job performance. And you can use those five to improve your company's profitability and motivate your new hire to fix problems that you were unable to fix yourself.

If done properly, a great Customer Experience Director can completely transform your client retention, improve your Net Promoter Scores, and dramatically improve your profitability within 6 months or less. Not to mention that they will take so much pride in their job that you'll have another amazing person on your leadership team who embodies the company culture and positive attitude that makes your company a great place to work.

Now that you have all the tools you need, I highly recommend that you put this book down right now and run your job post for your very first Customer Experience Director. Good luck!

Chapter 12

The Winners and Losers

Sometimes there are scenarios where there aren't any losers. When it comes to the remote work "game", this is definitely not one of those scenarios. There are certain people who are mentally incapable of adapting to a remote work environment which is one of the reasons why I call this incredible time period in human history an evolution. While it is unlikely that those who are incapable of adapting will literally "die off", it is certain that the value they bring to society will diminish. They will become much more dependent on the charity and goodwill of others and/or the government. As much as I would love to help these people, they have found themselves in a hopeless battle with modernity.

In this chapter, I'll talk about the winners and the losers of remote working and what will define each category. As an entrepreneur and a leader, it is imperative that you are able to identify who will make it and who will not so that you can build a great team and a lasting company. There are many pitfalls and dangers that all companies will face moving forward, but with the right team of highly adaptable people you can overcome anything. This chapter will show you how to pick those right people and avoid the wrong people.

The Zero-Sum Game of Remote Work

We live in a very interesting time, one where it often feels like we are in a battle between good vs evil, man vs woman, white vs black, and strong vs weak. As much as we have talked about the ambiguity that exists in present society, there is very little ambiguity when it comes to the battle between remote work and traditional in-house employment. This is very much a Zero-Sum game where there are winners and there are losers. There is little to no middle-ground here and it's up to you to ensure that you and your company survive. You must find a way to adapt your business in order to dominate your market in a remote environment and with a remote team, or you simply will not make it. We have already seen thousands of businesses, large and small alike, go under within just weeks of the pandemic here in the US. And I can guarantee that this trend will continue on indefinitely.

One of the reasons why this remote working trend will continue is because consumers and b2b brands will realize that they are now free to work with people all over the country and all over the world. No longer are you confined to working with the only accountant in your town or using the lawyer who always shows up at your Chamber of Commerce events. With improvements in technology, you won't even need to use local auto mechanics or doctors since in-home visits from mechanics and telemedicine will soon bring these services to your fingertips. You will have infinite options as to who you want serving you. All of this means that competition will get more fierce and the company with the stronger remote platform will win.

On the flip side, this also means that your local business will have more opportunities to work with new markets and new customers, who were previously unavailable because of geography. With the right remote strategy, the right remote team members, and the right remote infrastructure you can work with more clients than ever before. In theory, you should be able to be even more profitable since you can now drastically reduce your overhead. All of this future success is predicated on your ability to adapt. You must be willing to forget many of the things that helped you be successful before and reinvent yourself and your business. The rules of the game have changed, and the new rules are changing daily. The more quickly you can adapt, the more likely you are to emerge victorious.

Already we are seeing larger companies start to dominate and consolidate markets. For example, Amazon has all but solidified their dominance as the US's number one online marketplace. But niches will emerge within these industries that create more opportunities for the bold. For example, while Amazon is clearly the ecommerce leader in the US, a company called MercadoLibre. com is the dominating force for ecommerce in Latin America. Most Americans have never heard of this online retailer that has been growing and merging like crazy over the past decade, but they are now stronger and wider spread than even Amazon in Mexico, Central, and South America. Just think of all the undiscovered niches that are out there right now. Niches that you can jump into and help your company generate hundreds of thousands if not hundreds of millions of dollars for your business.

At the core of this success is more than just technology though. In fact, too much technology could cause your company to falter and miss the things that drive customers to stay with you forever. It always, always, always comes down to the customer experience. You must find ways to Bridge, Connect, and Deliver® throughout all stages of the customer lifecycle. You can find ways to do this with minimal tech and maximum human interaction to beat out any and all competitors. The company that can build the very best customer experience in a remote environment will win. Hands down. No questions asked. It is your job to make that happen.

Who Will Win

Let's talk about who will win this battle for survival in the remote working environment. So many companies today have lost sight of the importance of serving the customer. Americans have a history of forgetting the lessons that history has taught us. Ever since the Great Recession, our society has somehow buried the missteps that caused so many to lose everything. We have become so prosperous over the past 12 years that we started to believe our own bullshit and ultimately lost sight of the hallmark of a great business, that is the value it delivers to its customers. Our selfishness has become our downfall. But a great correction is coming. And whichever companies can deliver the best customer experience will prevail.

If you want to be one of the people who thrive, then you absolutely must obsess over providing best-in-class customer experiences. Bridge, Connect, and Deliver® are crucial to whatever strategy you choose because it helps you connect with customers no matter where they are. The beauty of Bridge, Connect, and Deliver® is that it works for all businesses, all staff, and all customers no matter where they are located. Sit down with your team and map out good, better, and best scenarios when it comes to customer experiences. Let your imaginations fly as if money was no option. You will be amazed at what you can create and the impact that it will have on your business in this new remote world.

A key aspect of customer experience that you must always focus on is how to make your customers lives easier. Many people today are struggling to adapt to today's challenges. Whether it be stressors at home or in the office, millions of Americans are looking for even the smallest outlets that can give them relief. This is why you must be able to recognize or anticipate what the challenges are for your customers and then deliver results that help them win the day. Empathy and love have never been more imperative than they are today.

You must surround yourself and build your company around empathetic people who can deliver these great experiences to your customers. Unfortunately, the level of empathy required to win has become absent in today's society, so you might find it challenging to find the right kind of team members. If you realize right now that you do not have the right people to build empathy-filled customer experiences, then my advice would be to start looking in places you never looked before. The best talent is undiscovered, and you can find it in places you never imagined. Look for people with different educational backgrounds, with different socioeconomic backgrounds, those who live in different countries, and even those who might not have the experience level that you once required. Company cultural shifts require personnel overhauls, so move outside your comfort zone and you'll find exactly who you need.

Finally, adaptation is paramount to your success, but not just adaptation to the marketplace and the requirements of remote work. Since your clients can now access you much more easily, that also means they can access your competitors too. You must adapt your service-offering and do what I call "own the board" to keep your customers from leaving you.

Imagine that your business is like a board game like Monopoly. In Monopoly, your objective is to own as much of the real estate on the board as possible. So in the context of your own business, owning the board means figuring out how you can adjust your customer experience and product offering so you are providing complimentary solutions to what you already offer and own as much "real estate" as possible. While specializing in one category (take Web Design and Development Outsourcing in my case) is crucial and you should always strive to be the #1 option in at least one main category, you must also look to fill other needs if you really want to own the board.

For example, at DUDE® we recognized that our clients require four main things to run their agencies. They need leads and customers for revenue, they need labor for fulfillment, they need mentorship for support and guidance, and they need technology to help them manage all the moving parts. This might seem overly simplistic, but based on the studies we've conducted, when you break it down, these are really the four main components that our digital agencies require to stay in business. Ultimately, this is our "board". In our quest to own the board, we have created DUDE® Leads to provide clients with lead generation, DUDE® (our core product) to help with fulfillment and operations, DUDE® School to help with mentorship, and finally we are developing more technology in addition to DUDE® Onboarding to give our clients the software that will help them run more efficiently. We realize that our board is constantly changing, and so we are always looking at ways we can adapt and create more ways to own our board.

Think about your own board and the different products and services you can create so that you can truly own the board. In the remote world, owning the board is so much easier because your clients are psychologically more eager and willing to work with a provider who can fill those gaps. You also have access to a greater talent pool who can help you create solutions so that your business owns the board.

What is your next move to conquer the board? Maybe it is taking a key team member and letting them create that product line they have always dreamed of. Or maybe it is merging with another company. Whatever your next move is, you must find ways to adapt and gain control of more of the board. If you can do this, you will not only survive this evolution, but you will dominate in ways you never thought possible.

Who Will Lose

The other day I was talking to a local digital marketing agency owner. He had done a very respectable job growing his agency in the local market. He had checked all the boxes for establishing himself as an expert in a little niche community. He had joined the Chamber of Commerce, gotten in good with the local business leaders, rented the fancy office, and built a team of in-house team members. It was the textbook way to win the pre-remote environment game. But his ego and his arrogance were sure to be his downfall.

This business owner had become so blinded by his past success and unwilling to adapt to a changing world that he could not see how close he was to being irrelevant. For one, he refused to work with anyone outside his local market. Two, he refused to update his packages and his pricing to compete for more of the board. And three, he refused to learn how to operate in a remote environment, going so far as refusing to allow his team members to work from home even during the height of the pandemic. Unfortunately, there are and will continue to be millions of people like this gentleman, whose own hubris will blind them to the need for swift adaptation.

If you are unable to adapt or are too slow to readjust to the shifting demands of the marketplace, then you have little chance of survival. Right now, we are all fighting for our lives, and those that stand still will die while those who are constantly on the move will survive. It's like Brad Pitt in the movie World War Z. If you stay in one place, you'll get eaten by the zombies. If you constantly move and adapt to the playing field, you have a much better chance for survival as the zombies (or in this case, your competition) will struggle to keep up with you. Will yourself to keep moving forward even if you are scared because if you do not keep moving the only other option is your demise.

Contrary to popular belief, a very small percentage of companies are totally incapable of operating remote. Many could save themselves, which is why I have such a violent reaction to people complaining that their business is "locked down" during this time. Sure, your job might be harder and certainly you'll have to make adjustments to the ways you operate, but most likely you can find a way to survive if you really adapt and persevere. However, that still leaves a small fragment of the business community who really will not make it, and it's not who you would think. The ones who are truly doomed to fail are the industries whose unique value proposition and customer experience is driven by face-to-face interaction.

Take an all-you-can-eat buffet for instance. An all-you-can-eat buffet's only differentiator from a regular restaurant is that you can eat as much as you want at no extra cost. Sometimes, like in Las Vegas, the buffets are an amalgamation of some of the most tasty foods on the planet, but more often, your average buffet is full of just average food. If you can't get that experience remotely, then the business is doomed. We already saw this with the closing of Souplantation/Tasty Fresh who closed their doors within two months of the pandemic. Without a complete overhaul of their business model and some very quick decisions on how to pivot, these few companies and industries will perish.

However, decision-making is another crucial indicator of who will survive the pandemic. It's very obvious that some people can not handle pressure. Remember Mike Glover and his belief that 10% of people will essentially ruin their chances of survival because they can't handle the stress? I'm sure we've all witnessed people who do insanely stupid shit when put under intense stress. And from what I've seen there are plenty of business owners in this boat. For the past decade, many people have amassed massive businesses without the luxury of having to be smart, brave, adaptable, or even good at their craft. Maybe their parents gifted them a business or maybe they just got lucky by being in the right place at the right time. Either way, if these individuals have not developed the skills and the tenacity to make good decisions quickly, by now they are really struggling. Freezing under pressure will lead to a swift death in this remote economy.

A leader usually only has 10% of the information that they wish they had in a difficult situation, but they still must figure out how to make the right decision. I've been put into situations like that before and I knew that if I made the wrong decision, it would have killed my business. To be honest, I had made bad decisions in the past that had killed past businesses, but those helped me learn how to make the right decisions with DUDE®. Regardless of whether you make the right decision or the wrong one, making no decision or taking too long to make a decision will always be the wrong decision. Those that can not seem to make decisions quickly will certainly be a casualty of the new evolution.

Another crucial mistake that will lead to the death of your company is not knowing your numbers. Warren Buffet said that when the tide goes out, you can see who isn't wearing their swimsuit. Well the tide is going out fast during the pandemic, and we are quickly seeing who is naked. In a "normal" financial crisis, you need to know your numbers beforehand so you can know what adjustments you must make to survive the crisis. However, this is a different kind of financial crisis since it's been created by a virus and so there are different numbers that you must know within your business if you wish to survive.

When I analyze a digital agency that is under performing or is having trouble hitting their goals, I usually will find problems in one of six areas. First, their Cost of Goods is way too high. In our industry, your COGS should not exceed 30% otherwise you will never have enough money to scale. Second, their Operating Expenses are too high. Maybe some people are getting paid way too much or they are spending money like drunken sailors on stupid shit. Third, they have really inconsistent sales. Fourth, their customer churn is way too high. Fifth, they are charging too little. Or sixth, they do not have the leadership team to help them solve problems and grow. Most often, the agency has problems in a combination of two of these areas. Very seldomly, they have problems in all of these areas.

It doesn't matter what industry you are in, for your own business you need to look at those same areas with the exception of sales. Why not sales? In this economy, you might not be able to increase sales that dramatically, or at least not very quickly, so you must figure out how to be more profitable in the other 5 categories. Also, if you focus on customer experience and client retention while simultaneously reducing your COGS and operating expenses, you'll find that you can run a much better business with far fewer clients.

This all starts with knowing your numbers though. If you're flying blind each month and essentially guessing what these figures are, you are going to fail. Eventually you'll hit a rough month or a rough quarter. And if you can't identify where the leaks in your boat are coming from, you'll quickly find yourself at the bottom of the Pacific Ocean. Whether you use a service like Bench.co or hire a full time accountant remotely, you must have perfect clarity on your numbers at all times. If you don't know the numbers, you're dead.

The final nail in your coffin is all about managing people. I have given you dozens of best practices about how to manage your remote team effectively, build an amazing company culture in a remote world, and dazzle your customers no matter where they or your team members are located. However, I know the sad reality is that a very small percentage of the people who read these words will actually take action. Most will fail to adapt or improve their leadership skills. For those people, management will be their biggest mistake.

If you can not properly manage your team members, then no matter how great your product or your pricing or packaging or whatever is, you will never survive this remote environment. Your best team members will leave to come work for people like me, your best clients will find a competitor who gives them the human touch that they crave, and your entire business will fall to pieces right before your eyes. All while you stand back helplessly, wondering what the fuck just happened. Sorry not sorry.

Business in the remote economy is very personal. You must Bridget, Connect, and Deliver on every level with your staff, and you must make this a major focal point of your management style. It's not enough to attract the people who are passionate about your mission and your clients, but you personally must lead them to greatness. If you can't do that, then you will die by the sword.

How to ensure you are a CHAMPION

If you're reading this, then I'm going to assume that you don't want to just win every once in a while. You don't want to bat .500

or be known as an average player. If you've read this far, then I can only assume you are looking to be a mother f**king champion. You want to be remembered as one of the greatest of all time. You want to be up there with Edison, Carnegie, Gates, Buffet, Bezos, and Musk. Well if there is ever a time for you to solidify yourself among those greats, this is it. You have all the tools at your disposal, and the playing field has never been more open for you to take over. This is your time, and you might never get another chance like you have today.

There is really just one thing that you need to obsess over day and night if you really want to build a massively successful, industry-dominating company during the remote working evolution. It is, and you probably knew this was coming, that you must absolutely crush it with Bridge, Connect, and Deliver® with customers and staff. Your people, processes, and products must scream Bridge, Connect, and Deliver® with every molecule of their being. That belief must be so powerful and overwhelming that your customers become evangelists of your brand. Your company culture will become so infectious that everyone wants to work for you, not because you pay more or because you give great perks, but because people know that the work you are doing is changing the world.

Bridge, Connect, and Deliver® is everything in remote environments. It is not just a slogan. Bridge, Connect, and Deliver® is religion. It is scripture. It is truth and beauty all rolled into one. If you can embrace this, then you will build an empire that people will talk about for centuries.

Chapter 13

Pants are overrated anyway

Congratulations! You have made it through 12 chapters and we are almost done. You have gone from a remote-working freshman to a PhD in remote economy. I always like to leave my readers with some very actionable content that you can implement and use to build a completely different business. And you should have all the motivation to do so as you also know why you must take action and the consequences of not adapting early. So for my final act, please enjoy this 30-day action plan that will set you up for greatness.

5 Things You MUST DO in the Next 30 Days

If you had to figure out a way for your company to change in the remote economy, there are thousands of things you could do. And we've already discussed quite a few in this book. But for now, I'm going to give you the five that you absolutely must do if you really want to be successful. I keep it at five because all of them are very achievable. I consider myself an expert on being able to predict who will be successful and who will not, and the thing that separates the winners and the losers is their speed of implementation. Most people will wait or say "I'll start that tomorrow". If you can't start implementing at least one of these tips by the end of the day, you're in trouble. I urge you to pick at least one and start it within the hour. This will give you the best chance of making it and will also make you a better business owner.

1) Turn on your cameras!

This is the first and most practical of all the tips. If there is anything you can do starting today, it's this one. One of the biggest benefits of meeting face-to-face is that you can read all the little body languages cues that people make, and it's much easier to ensure that everyone is understanding each other. We've all been in situations where you send a text message to a significant other and they infused a tone to your message, leading to a huge misunderstanding in which someone ends up sleeping on the couch. Take that scenario and apply it to a business setting. You could be losing thousands or millions of dollars without you even knowing it just because a customer misreads your meaning.

Leigh Thompson, professor at the Kellogg School of Management at Northwestern University, writes in her new book *"Negotiating the Sweetspot: The Art of Leaving Nothing on the Table"* that one of the biggest threats to companies in the remote world is the physical distance between team members and each other, as well as team members and customers. With Zoom and video calls being the main way we conduct business and interpersonal communication in the workplace, the research shows that by simply turning on your camera, you can dramatically improve the interpersonal connections between people. Seeing another human face during a conversation matters and it especially matters when you don't have the option to see that person in the real world in the first place. Turning on your video camera and showing your face humanizes you to the other person and helps you to Bridge, Connect, and Deliver® so that you build stronger bonds with customers and staff.

Furthermore, Thompson's research also shows that even if your customer has their camera OFF, you should have your camera turned ON during a video call. Since you have the ability to recognize your own facial expressions, seeing yourself during a call can encourage better control on the subtle aspects of verbal communication, like tone and amplitude, that can have a huge impact on how your message is received.

Think about how much more efficiently your company could run if your operations team and your customers never had a misunderstanding. How much money would that save you? How much more profitable would your company be? Also think about how much revenue you could generate if your potential customers trusted your sales people more? If the sales cycle was reduced by 25%, what would that do to your cash flow? This is how you have to analyze what happens the next time you and your staff keep your cameras off during a video call. The potential impact is massive so give yourself that added incremental chance to succeed and turn that camera on. Better to be safe than sorry, and the research shows that not only will you be safe, but you'll be a little wealthier too.

2) Be able to take money online

It is shocking to me how many businesses do not have the infrastructure to be able to accept payments online. It does not matter what type of business you are in, if you can't receive money from people anywhere on the planet, then you're losing that money. When you hear people whining that the "government shut down their business", what they are really saying is that they have not figured out a way to accept money from clients and distribute their goods or services virtually. In this day and age, accepting money remotely should be the easiest thing on earth, but for some reason many businesses still haven't figured this out. From PayPal to Stripe, there are literally thousands of ways to accept payments online. And if you need online document signing to compliment payment processing, then there are thousands of options for that, too.

You literally have zero excuses for not being able to take online payments from your clients. If you can accept money, then you stand a fighting chance. If you can't, then it's like walking into battle and trying to fight a tank with a slingshot. You have no chance of survival.

Here are a few ninja tips to help you win the online payment battle. First, you should create a subscription business for yourself. I have yet to find a business that does not have the capability to run a subscription payment plan for their customers. Whether that be a VIP level of service, unlimited consultations, or auto-deliveries, nearly every single company on earth can make this work. It's great because you get guaranteed revenue every single month and the clients get a better customer experience that in turn gives them some guarantees in a very uncertain world.

The second tip I have is to presell services. We are going to get through this pandemic and businesses will be able to have free-flowing, walk-in traffic again. Nobody can guarantee when that will happen, but it will happen eventually. If you presell your services at a discounted rate, then it not only gives your business a much-needed influx of cash and it also gives your clients hope and optimism that life will return back to normal one day. This influx of cash buys you time to reinvent your customer experience and thrive until the doors of society are open again for good. The packages that you presell can be redeemed when society is open again or maybe when a certain season hits. For example, Starbucks could presell pumpkin spice lattes to white girls if they really wanted to. You decide the best way for your business to presell your services.

Now, no matter if you choose to exercise both of those revenue-generating tactics or just one of them, there are thousands of businesses that are already utilizing these methods to survive and thrive. Don't fall behind the curve. Take action and make it happen.

3) Be able to communicate online

This should almost come before the ability to take money online because if you can't communicate effectively, then you probably won't be around very long. As I've talked about ad nauseum in this book, you must, must, must be able to communicate with your clients and staff at a level that you have never done before. You must create the systems and processes to ensure that communication in the remote world is super efficient. Far too often, I see companies kill their profitability because they have way too much unnecessary back-and-forth communication. All of these inefficiencies chip away at your profits. You must be able to get the highest quality product delivered to your clients in the fewest amount of steps, and unfortunately this is a massive challenge for most companies in the remote world.

Utilize the "Bridge, Connect, and Deliver®" philosophy to have open lines of communication with your clients and staff, and standardize communication across all levels to ensure that everyone is in a position to succeed. With in-house staff and in-person meetings, you could actually be more "sloppy" with your communication. If something didn't go right, you could just jump into the conference room or drive to your client's office and fix the issue. Those days are long gone. In the remote world, by the time you realize that bad communication has led to a problem, it's usually too late.

At the very least, in the remote world you must communicate with your new customers every single day to let them know how their project is progressing. People feel uncertain about everything, and a guaranteed way to reduce anxiety and give your customers some security is to over communicate. Let your customers know where they stand at all times and it will go a long way to creating happy clients. A simple email or better yet a phone call can make someone's day. This will force your staff to communicate better too because you have set the standards of communication and now everyone knows what needs to be done. In the end, you just need to be a human. Bridge, Connect, and Deliver® and everything will be much better for your company, your staff, and your clients.

4) Map out and deliver an amazing customer experience

This should be a no-brainer for you by now. Your customer experience is everything in the remote economy. You must sit down with your team and map out the customer experience for at least the first 2 years of a client working with you. This is the bare minimum if you want to successfully maintain and grow your customer base. If you don't do this, then your staff will not know how to meet and exceed your clients expectations. Without a plan, you will have unhappy customers, less revenue, higher expenses, and the risk of going out of business.

I recommend that you use the exercise that I outlined in Chapter 9 and sit down with your team to create 3 scenarios for the customer experience and the journey you want to take them on while they work for you. The first scenario is a "good" and realistic customer experience that you can very easily provide to your clients The second scenario that you have your team members map out is a "better" scenario, which is possible but that you probably would need to put a lot of time, energy, and money into. For example, maybe for their one-year anniversary you take the client to Disneyland or something like that. It's definitely do-able, but it will require a lot more planning and a bit more money. Finally for the third scenario, have your team pretend like money, connections, even the laws of physics are no option and have them create the most over-the-top, crazy customer experience imaginable. Pretend you could fly your clients around the sun or have a live, in-person concert with Freddy Mercury who you brought back from the dead for a special private concert. Literally, if they can imagine it then you write it down and have everyone present it.

When you finish with this exercise, you'll obviously have some ideas that are impossible to implement. But what's important is that you've gotten everyone excited about creating amazing experiences for the clients and have come up with new ideas that are actually really badass and would make your customers say "WOW!" Now, when you take this and factor in the elements of the experience that will need to be coordinated differently due to the physical restraints of remote working, you can really craft a customer experience that stands out from the crowd. This is what it's all about. Being creative and super intentional to make experiences for your clients that leave them feeling like you care about them more than you care about yourself. This is how you build community and lifelong customers who will never leave you, and this can be your reality with just a couple team meetings and a solid implementation plan.

5) Make sure you have the right people.

As Americans, we have been taught that all people are created equal. However, what Covid-19, quarantine, and the shift to a remote workforce has shown us is that not all people are equally capable of adapting. If you built your company with an "in-house first" mentality, then it's time to reevaluate and make sure you have the right people to help your business succeed in a remote environment. You must look at every team member and make sure that they align with what it takes to be successful today and in the near future. The sad reality is that not everyone is equipped with the mental and emotional skills required to make it in a remote work environment, and sometimes it's not even their fault. You can train these folks and try to bring them up to speed, but occasionally you have to make the very difficult decision that they just are not cut out for the new requirements. If you can't identify the people who are incapable of delivering for your customers and your company, then you risk having them doing irreparable damage to your business. I have witnessed first-hand how one person who is incapable of adapting can sabotage the operations and spread their cancerous beliefs throughout an organization.

The best way to ensure that you have the right people in the right seats is to first test all your staff. Give every team member a Psychometric Exam that is specific to their job role. The psychometric test will help you look at someone's values, beliefs, strengths, and weaknesses, which you can then use to gauge how well they may perform in a remote environment. I learned this from legendary investor, Ray Dalio, who used psychometric exams to build Bridgewater Associates from zero to $160 billion. Not that my company is worth anywhere near that, but the same hiring principles that Ray Dalio uses are similar to what we use at DUDE®, and they have helped us build an amazing company culture and thrive in spite of Covid-19. Identify the players that you need, evaluate the ones that you have, and make the moves necessary so that every person in your circle helps you survive.

The people you need on your team

Hopefully by now you're already thinking about the adjustments you need to make to your team. Maybe there are some people you need to add. Maybe there are people you need to "subtract". But in the end your team members are the most important aspect of your company. Your team members are even more important than the product you offer because if the market shifts, then the right team will help you figure out how to be successful and how to reinvent your business. In this section, I will show you the 3 people that you must have on your team if you want to crush it in the remote environment, and I'll even give you another job description that you can use to attract that new team member you are missing. These recommendations are all things that I have personally implemented at DUDE® so I know the impact that having any or all of these people on your team can make, not just to the bottom line but also how much fun you have in the business. Never forget that the wrong team can make you hate your life. However, the right team will give you a deeper sense of purpose and will make you excited to wake up everyday and take on the world. I'm not sure about you, but I'll choose the "right team" any day of the week.

Customer Experience Director

Surprise, surprise! If you're struggling with client satisfaction and customer churn, then the Customer Experience Director is the number one person that you need to hire today. Literally put the book down, take the job post I provided in Chapter 8, and run that shit right now. If you have problems in those categories, you need to face the cold, hard truth that YOU created those problems and now it's time for you to get out of the way so that someone else can come in and clean up your mess. Go back to Chapter 8, copy and paste the job description I provided, make the adjustments so that it fits your company requirements, and then run the job post. You can tell your existing staff about this new role and hopefully someone at your company will step up. Or if you have to find someone outside your company, it costs like $40 to run an ad on Craigslist, a couple hundred bucks on Indeed, or you can take the post and put it on your own personal Facebook page for FREE. The best part is that your new Customer Experience Director should pay for herself/himself within the first month by increasing your profitability, which makes this person a no-brainer.

Project Manager

I have always said that a good Project Manager is worth their weight in gold. A Project Manager helps bring balance and order between clients and team members. They are like the Jedi Master for your operations and customer experience. For those who have been operating as solopreneurs, the Project Manager is usually the first person that I advise them to hire since they will allow the owner to focus on solving higher-level problems that will take the business to the next level (and the owner SHOULD be working on these types of problems anyway).

The Project Manager is one of the most diplomatic teammates that you will have in your company. A great project manager has the unique ability to tell break the bad news to a client or coworker and yet the person on the receiving end will still love them for it. Great Project Managers are often born and not made, which makes them extremely hard to find. We use a combination of live 1-on-1 interviews, practical tests, the Psychometric Test, and live group interviews to find our amazing Project Managers. It took us a very long time to figure out this magic formula, but now we've got it down to a science.

Below you'll find our Project Manager job description, which you can use to attract great Project Managers for your own company. The last piece of advice that I'll give you about hiring this incredibly important person is to hire SLOWLY and TRUST YOUR GUT. Never force a round peg into a square hole and always listen to that voice in your head. If you do that, then you'll have a great chance of hiring a perfect Project Manager who will be a blessing to your company.

Project Manager Job Description

DUDE® is a binational company located in Tijuana, Mexico. We create design and development projects for digital marketing agencies in the US and Canada.

You can get to know more about our company by watching this video: https://youtu.be/KJ-d2nCx-Jo

We are looking for leaders with an excellent service attitude, who have worked as a developer or web designer, with at least one year of experience and fluent English.

Our work environment is relaxed and flexible. We offer our team competitive salary in different modalities, full-time and hourly freelancers, remote or office work, job stability and continuous opportunities for growth and professional development.

As a team leader, you will be the communication point between our clients and your work team. The team is made up of between 5-7 designers and developers, and your main tasks will be to keep clients updated on the status of their projects, assign tasks to the team, supervise and review the quality of each project, support all members, and make sure that everyone has what they need to carry out their functions. Evaluate, give feedback and give results to operations management.

These are the requirements to apply for this position:

1. Excellent time management, organization and service attitude
2. Minimum one year of experience in web design or development
3. Knowledge of HTML, CSS and Wordpress
4. Fluent English
5. Excellent time management, organization and service attitude
6. Leadership
7. Communication skills, proactivity and assertiveness
8. Effective problem solving
9. (Desirable but not essential) Experience in marketing platforms, e-commerce, mail, etc.

This is a full-time position and is in-person at our headquarters. If you are interested and you meet the requirements, send us an email with your CV, indicating the position "Pod Leader" in the subject of the email.

A better version of yourself

Of the three positions that I have mentioned, this is the one that I am the most excited to write about. Without a doubt, the improvements I have made on myself and my ability to become a better leader have made the biggest impact to my business and to my personal life. Like most owners, I initially hated the idea of hiring people. I always wondered why people couldn't "be as good as me" and wished that I could "clone myself". If you have ever said those words, I can definitely understand your pain. The reality is that nobody will ever be as good as you. But I have a newsflash for you: You're probably not as good as you think you are. Having the humility to understand that you're not the best, nor do you have to be the best, is one of the keys to being a great leader. Egos kill businesses so if you want to succeed in this new economy, then you need to remove the ego and reinvent yourself as a leader.

The most shocking point for me was when I realized that I was the problem and that the business was just a byproduct of my poor leadership. The issues in the business were really just symptoms of other problems that I had in my life. Every business person has said to themselves, "If I can just make more money, then everything else will be better". If I can make more money, then I can take my wife and kids on that vacation and we'll have a better relationship. If I can make more money, then I'll have more time to focus on myself and I can go to a therapist to deal with all that crap that happened to me in my childhood. If I can make more money, then I can hire a trainer and get rid of that giant tire hanging around my midsection. If I can make more money, I can have a better life! Don't get me wrong. Having more money can definitely solve a lot of problems, but the biggest thing keeping you from your big goals is how you THINK you achieve the big goal.

In my experience, the way you grow your wealth is to first fix your physical health, then fix your mental health, and then fix your relationships. When all three of those are going great and working how you want, then the money will flow. In short, you have to fix YOU if you want to grow the business. You must become a better leader beyond your company and in your personal life if you want to achieve your business and financial goals. The most important person that you need to hire if you truly want business success in the remote economy is the better version of yourself. I strongly believe that you already have all the answers to your problems inside your mind. It's your job to be the best leader possible so that those answers can come to the surface and you can make the improvements that will carry your company, your team, and your customers to never-before-seen levels of success. I urge you to look deep in the mirror at yourself and judge your leadership skills today versus what they could be with some major mindset shifts. Then all you have to do is make that ideal end product happen. When you can master new leadership skills, everything else will fall into place faster than you can imagine.

The people you need to let go

In this new world and with this new evolution, there are some folks you're going to lose and there are some people that you are going to have to leave behind. These could be employees who served you well up to this point, but unfortunately they have not been able to adapt to the new requirements of the mission so keeping them around jeopardizes everyone else. This is one of the most difficult parts of being a leader and is something that Jocko Willink spends a lot of time discussing in his bestselling book "Extreme Ownership". In summary, the leader has to know when you must cut ties with a team member, even if that person did all they could. Sometimes it's just not good enough and that's okay. It doesn't make you a bad person and it doesn't make them a bad person. You just have the rip off the bandaid and move on.

Here is the list of people that you'll need to let go if you want to survive this next evolution.

Those who are incapable of adapting

Adaptation is an interesting quality. When it comes to the ability for a human to adapt, some traits are nature and some are nurture. And the distribution of nature vs nurture is rarely the same between any two people. The Psychometric Exams that we have studied show that adaptability also changes depending on what stage of life you are in. Now this is not saying that age discrimination or any kind of discrimination is justified by any stretch of the imagination. What I am saying is that while someone might be qualified for a job today, they might not be tomorrow and vice versa. This is why it's so important to have an objective baseline, like the psychometric exam, so you can truly see who is incapable of adapting to a remote working environment.

Chances are you already have a strong inclination as to who these people are though. You already experienced them struggling to stay on task, they have repeatedly hampered or slowed down projects, and I'm willing to bet that they even know they aren't fit for the job anymore. If this is the case, then try to let them leave with dignity. Work together to create an exit plan and part in peace. I know that this is easier said than done, but if someone looks at the results from their psychometric, has seen the drop in their own performance, and is feeling unhappy, then most likely this will be a relief for the both of you.

Those who do not care about customer experience

I talk about this one specifically because it's been a big challenge in my own organization. I believe that certain institutions breed certain cultural beliefs and attitudes. For example, law schools tend to breed argumentative assholes (Just look at the difference between a first-year law student and a third-year law student). Or medical schools will tend to breed men who believe their shit doesn't stink and that they are God's gift to the world. In my industry, computer science and computer engineering programs tend to breed people who don't really care about the needs of other people. This can be extremely frustrating when you are looking to build a team of people who are inherently passionate about serving your clients, but nonetheless it must be done. You can not throw up your hands and give up on the importance of every single team member caring about the customer experience just because it's hard. You must find a way.

In our business, we typically get 42 resumes for every one developer that we hire. This means that 41 people who have the technical skills on paper, don't make it through the interview process because they weren't a good cultural fit. How many people are you interviewing before you make that offer letter?

No matter what, if someone in your organization does not care about the customers with the same passion that you demand from everyone else, that person has to go. If you have not stressed the importance of the customer experience to your staff prior to reading this book, you will most certainly have some push back when you bring up this mental and cultural shift. Those who think that their technical skills are more important than the happiness of the clients will reveal themselves and will try to undermine your new vision. I know this because it has happened to me and I've seen it happen to others, too. However, you should not be alarmed. All this does is make it easier for you to weed these employees out and remove them from your organization.

The easiest way to remove these problem children from your organization is to give them more tasks that involve customer experience. Do not expose your clients to these soon-to-be ex-team members, but have them do more customer experience training or create reports on the customer experience efforts that they are doing on a daily basis. Asking your team member to do this kind of work is like garlic to a vampire. In the end, you get the solution you are looking for and you won't have to worry about this problem employee much longer because they will soon quit.

The old version of yourself

If there is one piece of leadership advice that I want you to remember in this entire book, it is to stop looking outside yourself for all the answers. If you want to see different results in the business, then you need to change YOU. While that old version of yourself was fantastic up to this point, you are in a much different place and world now. So it's time for you to evolve and become the next version of yourself. This means that the old version of yourself needs to be "fired" so that you can hire this new badass CEO who has their shit together more than the last gal/guy. It's time to reinvent yourself and to embrace the mindset, attitude, and skills that will help you evolve and reach massive levels of success in this new world. There is literally nobody else who has more power to change the trajectory of your company than you do, and it all starts from within.

That old person who hated working remotely or believed that their business wouldn't survive if staff and customers couldn't come into the office needs to go "bye bye". The old boss who thought that technology was just a nuisance and couldn't really make a difference in the operations and profitability of the company needs to hit the road. The mistakes of the previous leader can not be repeated. The last leader refused to fire underperformers even though those employees neglected to update their skill sets. The last leader gave these employees countless opportunities, but they still couldn't become the people the company needed. And worst of all, the last leader didn't have the courage to cut the dead weight and get the ship back on course. These are no longer acceptable. You need to step into the new badass CEO role right away. If you can't find the courage to do this, then you might not have a company to lead in the months and years to come.

Taking the ship to Mars

Ever since Elon Musk announced his plans to take a group of brave humans to Mars, I wanted to be a part of it. The overall goals of his mission to Mars are pretty straightforward. Have a million human lives on the Red Planet by the year 2122, long after Musk is dead and in the twilight years for anyone who is alive today. Most astonishingly, he plans to have his first trip of cargo craft leave for Mars by 2022 and the first manned flight to Mars by 2024. The craziest thing about this entire plan? His company SpaceX is actually on track to do it.

So many have asked him, why Mars? Why leave the only planet that humanity has ever known for a giant, lifeless red dot that is 47.416 million miles away? Why risk the lives of 100 brave men and women, hurtling them through space for more than 150 days? Why Elon? Why???

According to the SpaceX website, Elon's answer is simple.

"You want to wake up in the morning and think the future is going to be great - and that's what being a spacefaring civilization is all about. It's about believing in the future and thinking that the future will be better than the past. And I can't think of anything more exciting than going out there and being among the stars."

Right now, even though it might not really feel like it, I think we are all out there among the stars. We are all hurtling through space, not sure if we will live or if we will die or what our new planet will look like by the end of the journey. The outcome of our world is uncertain and we don't know what the next month or year will look like. Humanity will most likely survive, but we do not know what our reality will look like and what casualties this latest evolution will leave behind.

The way I see it, you could live your life one of two ways. You can live in fear of the future and hide from the uncertainty in a tiny little cave on earth. Or you can embrace the excitement of the unknown and enjoy every minute on a crazy spaceship. I'm choosing the spaceship.

Remote working and this new economy are not going away. Those who say that life will return to the way it was prior to Covid-19 are delusional. We have moved far beyond the point of no return, and if anything, the future will make the world we knew before quarantine seem stranger than the one we have now. Just like Elon's rockets to Mars, this journey will be difficult, dangerous, and deadly for some, but there will be a lot of excitement for the ones who survive. That is the beauty of what we are experiencing today. If you survive, then the financial and personal rewards you gain from surviving this evolution will shape your life forever. It will be totally transformative and you will positively impact future generations. The best part is that after reading this book you will have a much better chance of success.

I urge you to burn the boats and march into the great unknown boldly and bravely. Embrace the uncertainty of the remote evolution and adapt quickly. Surround yourself with the people who also believe that if you Bridge, Connect, and Deliver® you can dazzle your clients, provide them with an experience better than they could possibly imagine, and ultimately change the world. Leave behind the actions of the past which will not serve you in the future. Make the hard decisions and become a better leader. The time and energy that you invest in yourself and in leading your team through this latest battle will pay off in the end.

When it comes to the decisions you need to make, go big or go home. If you continue doing what you were doing prior to the pandemic and you don't embrace the remote evolution, then your business is going to die anyway. You might as well give yourself a fighting chance and go all in. To have that chance of saving your business, you need to implement these changes NOW! As soon as you close this book, take action. Don't just hope or dream that things will change and not do anything about it. If you take the lessons that you learned in this book, you will have a much, much better chance of success. The reality is that you will most likely surpass your wildest dreams, your business will expand, and work will be more fun for you, your staff, and your customers. You will be a better leader and will help shape the lives of the people you lead.

I want to thank you for investing your time in reading this book. I spent countless hours researching and tens of thousands of hours amassing the practical experience that I have shared with you on these pages. If I can impact your life and help you grow your business, then all my past failures, all the long nights, and all the money lost have been worth it. Make me proud, make yourself proud, and go out there and make a difference. No matter what your "spaceship" is and no matter where your personal "Mars" is located, know you have the tools to get there, all while sitting in your home office and without the need for pants.

Bibliography

1. BlueZones.com, COVID-19:
Straight Answers from Top Epidemiologist Who Predicted the Pandemic

2 Parenting styles have changed but kids haven't
https://www.edge.org/response-detail/11859

3. Latchkey to helicopter parents
https://edition.cnn.com/2016/03/30/health/the-80s-latchkey-kid-helicopter-parent/index.html

4. Time Trends for Parenting and Outcomes for Young People
https://www.nuffieldfoundation.org/wp-content/uploads/2005/11/Time-trends-in-parenting-and-outcomes-for-young-people-vFINAL.pdf

5. Emergence of Stay-At-Home-Mom in 1980s
https://time.com/59807/stay-at-home-mothers/#:~:text=The%20phrase%20%E2%80%9Cstay% 2Dat%2D,at%20least%20the%20early%201800s.

6 Morris Rosenberg and the Rosenberg Self Esteem Scale
https://en.wikipedia.org/wiki/Self-esteem

7. John Vasconcellos and Public Policy aimed at growing self esteem.
https://en.wikipedia.org/wiki/Self-esteem

8. The Bad Things That Happen When People Can't Deal With Ambiguous Situations
https://www.thecut.com/2015/10/importance-of-dealing-with-ambiguity.html

9. The Essential Skill for Career Development – Dealing with Ambiguity
https://thetrainingassociates.com/blog/career-development-skill-ambiguity/

10. Dealing with Ambiguity – People Who Have Difficulty in Dealing with Ambiguity
https://strengthscape.com/dealing-with-ambiguity-people-who-have-difficulty-in-dealing-with-ambiguity/

11. How to Manage Someone Who Can't Handle Ambiguity
https://hbr.org/2015/03/how-to-manage-someone-who-cant-handle-ambiguity

12. The US Economy Since 1980
https://www.counterpunch.org/2007/09/29/the-us-economy-since-1980/

13. 27 charts that will change how you think about the American economy
https://www.vox.com/new-money/2016/10/10/12933426/27-charts-changing-economy

14. What's Going on With America's White People?
Trump's rise put a sudden spotlight on the troubles of white working-class Americans. A conversation with some of those who've been tracking them up close.
https://www.politico.com/magazine/story/2016/09/problems-white-people-america-society-class-race-214227

15. White Anxiety, and a President Ready to Address It
https://www.nytimes.com/2019/07/20/upshot/white-anxiety-trump.html

16. The Psychology Behind Sense Of Entitlement
https://www.betterhelp.com/advice/personality-disorders/the-psychology-behind-sense-of-entitlement/

17. American Exceptionalism and the Entitlement State
https://www.nationalaffairs.com/publications/detail/american-exceptionalism-and-the-entitlement-state

18. Creating Hostility and Conflict: Effects of Entitlement and Self-Image Goals
https://www.researchgate.net/publication/41401300_Creating_Hostility_and_Conflict_Effects_of_Entitlement_and_Self-Image_Goals

19. Linguistics scholars seek to determine what is unique and universal about the language we use, how it is acquired and the ways it changes over time. They consider language as a cultural, social and psychological phenomenon.
https://news.stanford.edu/2019/08/22/the-power-of-language-how-words-shape-people-culture/

20. How AI is seeing changes in stereotypes:
https://news.stanford.edu/2018/04/03/algorithms-reveal-changes-stereotypes/

21. German Bridges Are Girls, Spanish Bridges Are Boys
https://washingtoncitypaper.com/article/395742/german-bridges-are-girls-spanish-bridges-are-boys/

22. Two theories for this: Competition vs Identity and Self Esteem
https://www.psychologytoday.com/us/blog/finding-new-home/201908/the-psychology-us-vs-them

23. Psychological Safety: The History, Renaissance, and Future of an Interpersonal Construct
https://www.annualreviews.org/doi/full/10.1146/annurev-orgpsych-031413-091305

24. Forbes, Why A Culture of Us vs. Them is Deadly
https://www.forbes.com/sites/duenablomstrom1/2019/02/06/why-a-culture-of-us-vs-them-is-dea dly/#76da8eb97520

25. PGi, Why Remote Work Policies Fail Some Employers
https://www.pgi.com/blog/2017/07/why-remote-work-policies-fail-some-employers/

26. How to destroy the Us vs Them in VA culture
https://talentculture.com/how-to-move-people-past-an-us-versus-them-mindset-at-work/

27. Time Magazine, 'Superforecasters' Are Making Eerily Accurate Predictions About COVID-19. Our Leaders Could Learn From Their Approach
https://time.com/5848271/superforecasters-covid-19/

28. CNBC Coronavirus outbreak likely to go on for two years, scientists predict
https://www.cnbc.com/2020/05/01/coronavirus-pandemic-likely-to-last-for-two-years-scientists-pred ict.html

29. Washington Post, The next pandemic is already coming, unless humans change how we interact with wildlife, scientists say
https://www.washingtonpost.com/science/2020/04/03/coronavirus-wildlife-environment/

30. Financial Times, A bloodbath awaits commercial property investors
https://www.ft.com/content/739901a8-c601-4a81-b3e8-bb4f0eaa3e73

31. The Wall Street Journal, Coronavirus Triggers Steep Drop in New York City Commercial Property Sales
https://www.wsj.com/articles/coronavirus-triggers-steep-drop-in-new-york-city-commercial-property-sales- 11594047809

32. University of California, Milgram's Experiment on Obedience to Authority
https://nature.berkeley.edu/ucce50/ag-labor/7article/article35.htm

www.ingramcontent.com/pod-product-compliance
Lightning Source LLC
Chambersburg PA
CBHW031219050326
40689CB00009B/1393